Earth Mysteries of the Three Shires

by
Doug Pickford

CHURNET VALLEY BOOKS 1996

Published by
CHURNET VALLEY BOOKS
43 BATH STREET
LEEK
STAFFS ST13 6JQ

Copyright © D J Pickford 1996
ISBN 1 897949 16 2

Printed in Great Britain by the Ipswich Book Company, Suffolk

This book is dedicated to Hilary, my constant companion,
and to my father,
who has departed the Earth Plain but still visits.

There are many who have helped in many ways with the contents of this book. Their inspiration and dedication and their appreciation of the Land of the Three Shires has been invaluable and I am truly grateful to them - particularly those who encouraged me to continue with the Quest. They are too numerous to mention individually but please believe me: I will thank them face to face. Also thanks to the Alderley Mummers; Maurice Winnell (an invaluable source of help and inspiration), and the many I have met on my quests, including Andy Collins. If I have not given due credit to anyone then please forgive me. It is not intentional, it is forgetful.

By the same author:

Myths and Legends of East Cheshire and the Moorlands
Magic, Myth and Memories in and around the Peak District
Staffordshire: Its Magic & Mystery
Cheshire: Its Magic & Mystery
Treacle Town Treasures
A Portrait of Macclesfield
Macclesfield So Well Remembered
Macclesfield: Those Were The Days

Front cover:
Stone heads, a relic of the ancient Cult of the Head at Bakewell Parish Church.

CONTENTS

o DISLEY

WHALEY o
BRIDGE   o CHAPEL en le FRITH   HOPE

o   ALDERLEY

o MACCLESFIELD   o BUXTON   Gt. Longstone

Gawsworth

THREE SHIRE HEADS
                    X
o CONGLETON Wincle   BAKEWELL o

LONGNOR

Rushton   BUTTERTON o   o HARTINGTON

ENDON   o LEEK

WATERHOUSES
          o   o ILAM

An indication of the area within this book.

6

WHY THE LAND OF THE THREE SHIRES?

We have travelled around the Sun many times since I was initially encouraged to write my first book on what would now be given the overall title of 'Earth Mysteries'. At that period I was not too sure how it would be received, for the Age of Aquarius had certainly dawned but was being greeted with sleepy eyes. No fears of that today, for more and more good folk are appreciating not only what the Earth can give, but what has been stolen from the Earth. Today many of us can see a lot clearer.

This area centred on Three Shires Head - that wild moorland spot where the Celtic Water Goddess still lurks - is now used as a human mark or boundary place: the three Shires of Cheshire, Staffordshire and Derbyshire. They may now be separate Counties but they are still unified with myths, legends, magic and mystery. Now, three books later, I am delighted to be able to return here to my 'roots' and take a fresh look at yet more local mysteries of the Earth, magic of the Moors and myths of the Moment with new information that has come to light. This is a completely new book with completely new Quests within and although I and many others have not, yet, fully discovered all those Holy Grails we seek we are getting nearer: for this is the Land that holds so many surprises and most of them are, I am pleased to say, pleasant. It is the Land that centres on the townships of Macclesfield, Buxton and Leek and stretches as far West as Alderley and over towards Bakewell in the East (not forgetting delightful Bear Town - Congleton - to the Southwest).

One of the many pleasing aspects of writing and researching my books has been the response that has ensued from readers. I have been shown many natures of this wonderful area I did not know existed and I have been sent on journeys that have proved extremely fruitful. It is mainly as a result of these people, many of whom I am pleased to now be able to count as good friends, that I have been able to collect more than enough information for another book. And here it is. In earlier publications I thought it necessary to explain what 'Earth Mysteries' were all about. I thought it would be advisable to describe how some people could see the Lie of the Land with their Sixth Sense or their Third Eye and how the Ancients were aware of Knowledge that became suppressed and swept under the proverbial carpet. But not any more, I feel, for I am now of the knowledge of a vast number of good people out there who are not only appreciative of the magic within this Land of the Three Shires but have contributed to it.

I have, as a result of writing these books, had the pleasure of meeting Mediums, Dowsers, Ghost Hunters, Wiccas, Wise Men and Wise Women, Worshippers of Trees and Worshippers of Rocks, not to mention those who take healing from the land, water and air and those who give healing. I have also had the pleasure of meeting many who keep alive traditions of old such as the Alderley Mummers and groups of people who still meet, albeit secretly, at that magical, mysterious and marvellous place we now call the Edge at Alderley. I have had the honour of being invited to the ritual lighting of Beltaine Fires and also to the celebration of ancient Samhain (now Hallowe'en) at a magical and mystical site in Derbyshire. I have been escorted across mountain and moorland, peak and plain and town and village by people wishing to show me this mystery or that particular object and have been made welcome in, among other places, remote farmhouses in Derbyshire, luxurious homes in Cheshire and homely homes in Staffordshire. Within those walls I have been told many secrets. The more I have discovered about this Land of the Three Shires the more I marvel about this unique area and the unique people who have inhabited it. And who still do. This is the area that, once in your blood, will never leave. It draws like a magnet. It never lets go.

Shortly after my Peak District book appeared I was asked to give a talk to a group of people in the Staffordshire Moorlands town of Leek. I was uncertain of how many would turn up, and thought an audience of thirty something would be very nice indeed. However, such was the interest in the topic of local Earth Mysteries within and around that very special town that well over two hundred hardy folk turned up on a cold January night. Unfortunately many had to be turned away because there was, physically, no more room for them at the inn (the Swan on St Edward Street) but as a result of that evening an Earth Mysteries Group was formed and called the Green Dragon Mysteries Society that has, at the time of writing, one of the largest - if not THE largest - memberships of such a club or society in the entire United Kingdom and has attracted many famous speakers. And these speakers, more often than not, ask to come to this Society, such is its fame. But that's not all. Macclesfield, too, is inhabited by many who appreciate the Old Ways and I had the great honour of being asked to be inaugural speaker at a meeting organised by some of these folk, for which I thank them. Here in Treacle Town such was the vast interest in the subject that tickets rapidly sold out and many people had to be turned away. And at Buxton there has long been such a Society - the Buxton Psychic Group - and among its members are many talented and sincere people who have long been aware of the area's magic and mystery. When Graham Phillips and Andrew Collins (two internationally renowned authors) visited the Leek club in 1994 they were both amazed at the size of the audience. They shouldn't have been for both of them have written about mysterious aspects of this area around the Three Shires and they keep returning to it - drawn by its magnetism. They, like so many others, are aware of the special nature of the place. Is it, therefore, surprising that the people who inhabit the Land should be so interested in its uniqueness? I think not.

Hardly a week has gone by without some new aspect of the Land of the Three Shires being brought to my notice. It is primarily these many varied and exciting revelations that are highlighted within the pages ahead. I have been told a lot I was not aware of. For instance, in my first book I highlighted a ley line that goes from the Parish Church of St Edward the Confessor at Leek to a stone circle just outside Rainow beyond Macclesfield and I have subsequently been told (and shown) that, in addition to a number of special mystical and magical places and objects that I mentioned could be found along that line, there is a marker stone by the side of Blue Boar Farm to the East of Rainow village and situated directly upon that very special earth energy route. And that line also travels through a tumulus or burial mound, also at Rainow. So yet another thread in life's rich tapestry has been woven. And in this book I sincerely hope I am able to weave some more. In this latest work, as previously, I endeavour to ask questions. Sometimes answers do not readily come. Sometimes they do. Please ask your own questions and please go on your own Quests for the hidden treasures still waiting to be discovered. There is an elegance of riches within this Land of the Three Shires and I am delighted to share these newly rediscovered delights with you.

I have greatly enjoyed writing and researching this book. I sincerely hope you enjoy not only reading it, but carrying out your own voyages of discovery. Included is a sketch map of the area this book roughly covers. Each strand is interwoven with another to make the rich web that it is and, hopefully, you will discover more of what it will yield. Happy hunting!

1
THE CRYSTAL MAZE

Tony Hibbert is a retired craftsman whose delight is walking the wild moorland above the Goyt Valley. I first met him when I was giving a talk in Macclesfield and he and his good lady were sitting in the front row by the aisle. I was setting up my projector and as I did so we chatted about this, that and the other. After I had concluded my talk and slide show on the magic and mysteries of the area, including my meeting with the witches of Alderley Edge, he approached me and asked if I knew about what he termed a "strange stone" close to Pym Chair high above the Goyt Valley. In fact this was the first time I had heard anything about it and Tony extended the invitation to take me to see it - which I readily accepted.

November is usually a misty month but on that particular day shortly after All Hallows Eve of 1994 when I accompanied him to Pym Chair, and then across the moors, the sun shone proudly. Tony is a tall man and he strode out with gusto, his walking stick in his right hand. We hiked to Oldgate Nick and beyond in search of this strange stone but, alas, it did not wish to reveal itself to us. That particular moorland, like most, is overgrown with bracken and with bilberry or wimberry bushes and that particular stone on that particular day was determined it was not going to be found. I and Tony scanned the area high and low, walking every inch of the moorland but its secrets were hiding. He was determined not to be beaten for he had seen this stone only days before and he trudged up, down and across and around. But it was not to be.

However, I had the feeling that we had not gone there for nothing and although on the surface it looked a fruitless venture something was telling me not to give up. Tony certainly wasn't going to give up and after a half hour or so he shouted to me. "Come here, Doug." His voice rang across the moor. I trekked towards him and as I got nearer I heard him say, "Tell me what you make of this."

He was standing by a small mound that looked, from a distance, like an ancient burial site. As I got nearer I saw that just off centre of the mound was a small circle of stones and within that circle had been placed a host of tiny crystals about the size of some sweets I remember having as a child - we used to call them "Hundreds and Thousands" - do they still make them? There were hundreds, if not thousands, of these small crystals within this circle of rocks or stones more or less on the top of this mound and we both stood and stared.

What was the significance of this man-made structure? This wasn't the sight Tony had brought me to that high moor to see on that particular afternoon but it was an intriguing one, nevertheless.

The stones we discovered. Within them were hundreds and thousands of small quartz 'chippings'. Why had they been placed on this strong ley line?

As we began to examine the extraordinary structure something occurred to me. I had seen something like it before and not all that far away, either. Let me explain.

Those of you who have read Myths and Legends of East Cheshire and the Moorlands may recall the tale I told of my son Charles and a good friend of mine named Mike Oldham, plus myself, following a ley line, earth energy line, dragon line or whatever you wish to call it, from the Parish Church of St Edward the Confessor in Leek through Macclesfield Forest and concluding at a stone circle within a clump of trees close to Rainow. In the centre of that site where the energy flow ceased someone had erected a small circle of stones identical to the one that Tony had stumbled across. Inside that particular circle was a wreath of holly, ivy and mistletoe reminiscent of the Druidic beliefs of old. But inside this one in the Goyt Valley there was not any wreath - just hundreds and thousands of small crystals. But why?

I usually never go anywhere without some dowsing rods being close to hand but on this particular occasion I had not brought any (isn't it always the case?) and so was not able to do any investigations into possible ley lines around this site. I would have been very, very, surprised if this wasn't something to do with these energy lines, however, and resolved to return as soon as possible to investigate further.

The following Sunday I and my wife Hilary were out and about in the car. We have a list as long as our arms of places to go and people to see and as every moment of our free time is precious to us we try to make the most of our outings. I mentioned to her about the find on the moors above the Goyt Valley and we both agreed this should be top of the list to visit. Again, those who have read previous works may possibly be aware that Hilary is a talented Medium (and I will embarrass her further by mentioning she is a very talented Healer also) and she has often assisted my Quests by seeing that which should have been patently obvious. She would be ideal, thought I, to help unravel this mystery.

We drove up towards Pym Chair from that ancient site of worship now known as Jenkin Chapel and as we did so the land became more and more enveloped in mist. By the time we reached the summit visibility was at a minimum, but nevertheless the morning was full of magic and we were happy to be there. We were, in fact, not alone in being happy and sensing the magic of the place for as we walked along the ridge path we heard the strains of several voices singing away. As the voices got nearer we realised they were singing for sheer enjoyment. They were free and happy. Soon we saw shapes emerge from the mist heading towards us and we made them out to be young lads, teenagers, who had been walking as free men on Sunday just like the Manchester Ramblers in the folk song trudging the moorland. They were singing because they wanted to and because they were happy to do and as they walked by they showed no embarrassment at all. They were singing with gusto 'I Love to Go a Wandering'. Hardly Street Cred but what the Hell!

I took Hilary to the stones containing the crystals and her immediate impression was confirmation that the site was an ancient burial mound. The quartz had not been there all that long but they were marking a VERY strong ley line. Just where it came from, however, it was not easy to discover that morning because visibility was at a complete minimum. Another time, maybe. It was something to look forward to.

My next visit to the site was with Maurice Winnell. Maurice is a Macclesfield resident who has accompanied me on many investigations in and around our Three Shires. He had taken part in many archaeological 'digs' in the 60s and 70s at local burial mounds and it was he who taught me how to spot a tumulus. In return I taught him how to dowse. He is very knowledgeable on all aspects of ancient history and has compiled a unique list of all the known ancient sites within the area.

Our visit to the Goyt Valley moors, in particular that mysterious group of stones filled with quartz, coincided with a bright and sunny day just right for dowsing and for following any ancient paths we may be led to.

We parked at one of the official car parks at the top of the hill and walked the path by the side of the road until we crossed over to the stile that takes the walker along by a drystone wall. In the stones on the ground by the stile there are carved two initials, 'P C'. Obviously at some time someone has decided to place them there to commemorate the fact that the area is known as Pym, or Pym's, Chair and right by them is a 'trig' mark. Perhaps one and the same mason chipped both. I have speculated long and laboriously on the origins of the name Pym Chair in the book *Magic, Myth and Memories* and must not repeat myself here. We went through the stile and along the path by the drystone wall, re-built by a craftsman, and up towards that part of this magical land known as Cat's Tor (the hill of battle) and the vicinity of Shining Tor, the lofty summit named because of its associations with the Shining Ones, the gods of old. But on this occasion we do not journey to the peak of the gods, we pause when we reach Oldgate (or Old Gate) Nick to our right. This is now just a break in the rock face a distance of one third of a mile or so from Pym Chair. There is a distinctive nick in the top of the ridge; a nick that is, indeed, visible from parts of Macclesfield. It can be seen from Prestbury Road as you walk from Dale Brow House to the lane ends at Fallibroome. There are some bold rocks here that make a clear cut line against the sky and the name 'gate' does, to my way of thinking, imply a way through, a street or road, from the Norse 'gata'. Thus Old Gate Nick means the old way through.

Look left as you stand by the Nick. There is the remains of an old road, an ancient way through - a way as old as time. It is down this ancient path we head towards our small stone circle but before we do, let us pause and speculate about this ancient way. It does, I think, have associations with the highway nearby that runs along by Pym Chair that is known as the Street, said to be a Roman Road, for its direction appears to head that way before being lost on the moorland. It was, I feel, an old route leading to another old route - the Street. Yes, the Romans utilised this road but I suspect it was there before their time. The Street is still in evidence and carries a latinised name from 'strata' but the other ancient route through the Nick is all but lost. It can still be made out and was a highway that must have carried much traffic at some point in its history because of its width. Let us hope its memory, at least, remains with us.

But to return to our crystal circle: turning left at The Nick we followed the old road down the moor (and here I must point out that it is not now a designated path so I advise and urge both respect for the land and for the owner of the field, although it had been a way for thousands of years - please do not stray from the pathways, especially at lambing time, the area of the circle can be viewed from the ridge). Dowsing rods showed there was not just one ley line at the point but a number of them, radiating like the spokes on a cycle wheel but there was one that was enormous in its strength. It was generating energy over towards the Goyt Valley and so we decided to line up the energy path on the map and also to confirm its direction by sighting on the horizon with the idea of following it to we knew not where.

A brief spurt down the road in the car towards the Valley brought us to a small lay-by on our right where a stile shows the footpath to Errwood Hall, a route used and enjoyed by countless thousands. Our line crossed this path and went up the hill and we

The standing stone on the ley line, perched over a spring. It can be found on the footpath to the left of the track used to take walkers to Errwood Hall's remains. At some time it has been pushed, or has fallen, over.

17

noticed something that looked very interesting - a lone standing stone on the side of the hill. We could not confirm at that moment that the ley line passed through it but we rather hoped it would. There are many of these ley markers throughout the land. Some are now boundary stones and some are just marks on the landscape because the earth energy has gone - either moved by man or by Mother Earth.

We walked towards it and began to pick up the strong ley line again and, sure enough, it passed through this standing stone. The stone itself has toppled somewhat, either through the erosion of time or because of help from a human being or two. It has not been uncommon in the past to topple these stones during fits of religious fervour. Most of the so-called stone 'crosses' at churchyards throughout the area are witness to this. Puritan zeal ensured very few of them were allowed to remain intact. However, this stone was obviously something very special indeed. Beneath it, on the side facing Pym Chair, there was a patch of mud and our first thought was this had been made by sheep sheltering from the wild winds that can rage up there but further thought and investigation showed this not to be the case. The mud was there for a very good reason - a spring was oozing from under it.

Not only was the stone marking the path of a ley line it was marking the site of a spring - a spring that was being strengthened by the unique and still mysterious properties of an energy line within the earth. We now had two points on the map to line up and drawing a line in pencil showed us that it carried on through what is now Errwood Reservoir and over towards the very aptly named Wild Moor. We drove through the valley where even on a wintry day there were many enjoying its beauty and up towards the Wild Moor, towards the shrine further on erected by the last occupants of Errwood Hall.

This shrine still attracts pilgrims. More often than not flowers

18

are to be seen within its protective stones and they seem to last for a very long time; whether this is the preservative qualities of faith or the icy winds I leave to you. It is not on the line we are now following but, quite interestingly, is upon an energy line - surprising, because those who built it were devout Christians.

Village of stone on the wild moor

The car park at the top of the hill, by the old railway line that is now an excellent walkway, was a perfect place for our continued exploration of the energy path that started with the formation of stones containing quartz perched on a possible ancient burial mound near to Oldgate Nick. There are many paths across this bleak, blustery and beautiful moor that lies across the road from this car park. The area is sometimes known as Wildstonemoor, with the brook babbling below. It has been criss-crossed by pack horse trails in its time and its beauty is now in its desolation and isolation. There are still the ghosts of these jaggers walking with their mules, bells tinkling round the animals' necks, across this bleak spot. You can see them if you look strongly enough. Please enjoy this wonderful place for what it is - one of the many uplifting places around this enchanting area.

Our ley line crosses the brook or stream and goes across the moor towards Buxton. As we followed the pathways down to the valley scooped out by the waters flowing through, Maurice noticed a pile of rocks or stones. Nothing unusual in that, but they were not in a natural formation, they were oval or circular. And then there was another set. And another and another. These stones, half way down the valley, were slap bang on our energy line and had been placed there for a purpose. It was Maurice who had first drawn my attention to the Iron Age village atop Bosley Cloud - *Staffordshire: its Magic and Mystery* - with circular dugouts of stone and he pointed out the similarities here. There is no doubt at all that these stones were once part of a very old centre

19

Some of the stones on Wildstonemoor. They have undoubtedly formed inhabited structures at some time. Some say they are quite recent but others are of the opinion that they stretch back for countless centuries. Work with a pendulum and dowsing showed that there had been 'habitation' here at least two thousand years ago. They are situated on the energy line.

of habitation and they are on the powerful ley line.

The line carries on through Buxton Golf Course - of which Maurice is a member, incidentally - through the park by the Pavilion Gardens and then to Staden Low and a tumulus beyond at King Sterndale. Low or Lowe means either a hill, or burial mound (I am inclined to say it means a burial mound more often than not atop a hill) and these sites were without fail on an earth energy line, presumably in the belief of regeneration or rejuvenation by the properties contained within the line. Just what powers these lines contain has been speculated upon for many years and many 'scientists' poo-poo the idea that they exist. They do exist, they are not imagined. Our ancestors knew of them, for every ancient site in this country stands on or near one, but the knowledge of them was suppressed for many centuries. It is only during the twentieth century that people have come out of the closet and once more admitted they believe of their existence. There is perhaps now no fear of physical injury for stating this belief, as there used to be in times past, but perhaps there are still certain elements of our society who would like to pillory those who admit to understanding them. It is very sad.

But let us return for a while to the mystery of our small stone circle. It has undoubtedly been placed there for a purpose - but what is, or was, that purpose? Is it a complete and utter coincidence that this spot should mark not only the end of one of the strongest and largest ley lines in this area, but also mark the spot where several others converge? Perhaps.

Is it also a coincidence that this spot happens to be, in all probability, the site of a cairn or ancient burial? Perhaps.

Is this small circle of stones a completely natural construction? Perhaps.

Is it just a complete coincidence that it happens to be the same size and of the same construction as the one previously discovered at Rainow? Perhaps.

And what is the significance of the hundreds and thousands of tiny quartz stones? Did they find their own way there? Perhaps they did - but that would be stretching probability to the extreme. Coincidence is undoubtedly a possibility and I am a strong believer in meaningful coincidence as Jung described and named 'syncronicity'. Probably the only real certainty is that the crystals were taken there but surely this site was chosen for a specific reason and purpose. Just who and just why is the uncertainty although whoever built that circle on that site knew it was a special spot and may very well have been aware of the ley lines therein. If that should be the case (and if I was a betting person I'd certainly put my money on it) then we've got to assume that the crystals have a special significance.

Crystals are significant in many ways. It is indeed a fact that most houses that are purported to be haunted are constructed of stone containing a high proportion of quartz crystal and perhaps it is this substance that retains memories and could be a reason for the psychic pictures of what has taken place being seen again, particularly powerful incidents (murders, suicides, etc) being recalled. The art of scrying - foretelling the future - is also called crystal gazing. Today, crystals are being used more and more for healing and they can also be found on the end of many a pendulum. Most stone circles and monoliths are constructed of stone containing crystal - particularly quartz. There is a strong belief that crystals can soak up energy in the form of thought waves and psychic energy and there is also a powerful belief that the energy contained within ley lines - used for healing purposes by some - can be retained in crystals, rather like a battery.

Could this be the reason for the placing of crystals at our tiny circle of stones above the valley of the River Goyt? It's possible and short of someone coming forward and saying, "Yes, I constructed this circle and placed the crystals in it," and giving another reason, probably a very plausible one once we hear it, then it's one of the best bets we've got.

There is another possibility, of course. It could have been placed there to heal a 'black' energy line. There certainly are lines within our earth's surface that have been damaged, perhaps through quarrying or the laying of massive electricity cables or the construction of a motorway or whatever and these are known, in some cases, as 'black' lines for their powerful positive energy has become negative.

Only weeks after I had seen the small stone circle in the Goyt Valley for the first time I was asked to visit a lovely house on the

Staffordshire and Cheshire borders to see whether there was such a black line going through it. There was a problem with cancer, or the possibility of a problem, for one of the occupants and they wished to know whether they were living on a black line. Their neighbour had suffered the terrible disease and this accentuated their fears.

They were, indeed, living on an earth energy line but they were on a positive one and their fears were totally groundless. The expression on their faces when I told them the news was a joy to behold and I shall never forget it. So how can anyone tell whether a line is 'black' or 'white'? Quite easily, just go there and it's like walking through the front door of a house you've never visited before: you either instantly feel 'at home' in the house, or in the area you are visiting, or you don't. Sometimes you feel downright uncomfortable. It's not, usually, very easy to produce dowsing rods and ask to walk up and down the lounge or trample across the back lawn in search of black or white lines, but if you're able to then the dowsing rods will tell you whether there's a good or bad line - if you ask them. Mind you, if your initial instinct or senses have already told you that everything is fine then, ninety nine times out of a hundred, all IS fine.

There was, in the 1970s, a village in Cheshire that had an undue number of deaths and illnesses because of the awful disease of cancer and a good friend of mine was asked by a number of residents to see if there was anything untoward within the earth that could be a reason for this outbreak. There was. Quarrying of a hill overlooking the normally peaceful place had changed the structure of an energy line from good to bad, he discovered. The village church had, most probably, been built on the 'good' line many hundreds of years ago and, no doubt, that church had been built on a temple used by the so-called 'heathens' before that and these people had built their temple there for a reason - because it was on a line of energy. Unfortunately our modern methods of scooping out the earth to extract minerals or whatever had now worked against the inhabitants.

My friend had two courses open to him. He could either divert the energy line with metal rods stuck into the earth or he could use crystals. On this occasion he chose to use metal rods - some six feet in length and quite thick - and, with the aid of a JCB excavator and a few farmers he drove the rods into the ground along the energy line. He used the bucket on the excavator just like a mighty hammer - the god Thor using his power for the good of his earthly followers! In doing this he formed an 'ever-decreasing circle' and the line was diverted round and round until it went down into the ground rather like water down a plug hole. As long as those metal rods are there this line should continue to do just that. The last time I passed through the village I made a detour to check if they were untouched and I saw them in the ground. Please appreciate that I am not hiding the identity of this village for any other reason than to save the residents undue embarrassment and, quite possibly, distress. I have worked on newspapers for long enough to appreciate what can come about through undue publicity. And as for the inhabitants of the village - while there were no instant cures, a number did recover and the instances of people contracting this affliction are now more or less average. As I always say, perhaps it is a complete coincidence. And perhaps not.

If he had decided to use crystals for the purpose of 'healing' the line he could have placed a goodly number of them on the line itself and they would have absorbed the energy which, in this instance, was a negative energy. Or he could have used them to divert the line just as he did with the metal rods.

Had the quartz crystals in the Goyt Valley been placed there for this reason? Or had they been placed there because the line was a positive one and they were absorbing the good that comes from this energy?

Perhaps there are other structures housing crystals around this area. If you are aware of one, then please let me know, and if you are responsible for placing that circle where it is, then please get in touch. I can honour a request to keep it quiet, I can assure you! I am certain that one day we will be able to solve this tantalising mystery and I am equally certain that there will be many more mysteries to unravel and interesting people to meet in the process.

The frightening power of thirteen

This area around Pym Chair is one that contains many mysteries. Perhaps, for instance, you may recall my mentioning the mystery of the millions upon millions of caterpillars that descended on the area during the First World War? Some thought they had been dropped from a German Zeppelin and others thought they were a heaven-sent plague - and a Curate from Macclesfield who set about investigating the mystery later met his end when he was travelling to the Amazon where he was to become a missionary. As a result of my mentioning this in the Peak District book, I received a letter from a lady, Mrs Hall, living at Tower Hill, Rainow. She had spoken to me when I was at a book-signing session at W H Smith's and told me she had a letter half-written to me and she would hopefully finish the other half. I received her finished letter shortly afterwards and it read:

"I was most interested in the story of the caterpillars. In it you wrote about the Reverend Vyvyan Kingdom who had been sent from St Peter's to Rainow parish during the war. My grandfather, Mr A E Lea, was a dentist who lived and had his surgery on Park Green, Macclesfield. He was on one side of the archway and Bibby the plumber was on the other side. My grandfather was a long-standing Church Warden at St Peter's and my mother, Ida, used to tell me the story about when the Rev Kingdom was due to take up his new position as missionary in the

25

Amazon. My grandfather and grandmother arranged to have a farewell supper for him at their home. Both the Rev Kingdom and the Vicar of St Peter's, the Rev Cholmondley James and one or two other church wardens were invited. My mother was one of five children and they were all to attend the supper. As they were about to sit down for the meal my grandfather pointed out that there would by 13 seated round one table and being very superstitious he was not happy and wanted to split the party onto two tables.

The Rev Kingdom would have none of this and said they must all eat together, he was not the least bit worried, and they apparently all had a very entertaining evening. It was only a few weeks later that they were informed of the Rev Kingdom's untimely death and to his dying day my grandfather blamed the fact that thirteen people having shared the same table had brought this about."

Why should thirteen people around a table be thought to be unlucky? I remember once being on a radio phone-in programme and being asked that very question by a listener. The best reason I could give at the time was that at the Last Supper there were thirteen people around the table. I still think that is the main reason but there was also the belief at one time that anything above 12 was of the unknown and so the Entrance to the Unknown was therefore the number 13. This is why we used to add in dozens before decimalisation and the unhappy schoolchild had to learn tables up to "12 times 12 equals 144". We never went beyond that, remember? One of the oldest forms of adding on a hand takes us up to the number 12 - just hold out your hand, palm uppermost, and use your thumb as the counter. Then, starting with the index finger next to the thumb count the digits and then the digits on the next hand and so on. They make twelve. Anything beyond that would be unnatural.

The caterpillar plague occurred at the area around Greenstacks Farm. Just above this farm there stands the rocky outcrop known as Windgather Rocks, separating the boundaries of Cheshire and Derbyshire where, incidentally, there is yet another very strong ley line. Perhaps dowsers may like to try and find this

What is the secret of this circle carved into a rock below Windgather Rocks? Some think it is connected with the tales of a gibbet that is said to have been there at one time. As the area is on the boundaries of Derbyshire and Cheshire there may have been such a structure where felons, perhaps those who tried to use the escape of racing into another Shire from the one they committed their offence in, were left to hang as a warning to others. Another theory is that it was a sighting point, reflecting the sun when filled with water. These sighting points were, and are, often found on earth energy lines or ley lines. A strong line exists from Windgather Rocks (try to pick it up as you walk along the footpath that straddles the tops of the Rocks) to the Derbyshire hills. Whatever the reason, this circle has been carved there for a very good reason but time has, I feel, lost the answer.

one, it can be readily discovered by keeping to the footpath that goes across the backbone of these rocks. It has been said that hangings used to take place on these rocks but nowadays it is merely the rock climber and the rambler who have the biggest use for them. Their situation, enjoying panoramic views across Derbyshire and a great part of Cheshire must mean that, strategically, they have played a significant part in our history and there are the remnants of some carvings in the millstone grit rock face that have now all but worn away and cannot be identified satisfactorily. A great shame. There has also taken place a good deal of quarrying over the years and this must have put paid to some clues to the past.

In front of these imposing rocks that are so aptly named (the wind gathering with gusto around them), there is one flat stone that has a circular hole carved in to it.

The significance of this is tantalising. It looks like it could have had a pole stuck in to it (for the gallows or gibbet, maybe?) or it could have been used simply to gather a small pool of water for ceremonial purposes or, when the sun reflects into it, as a sighting mark. Then again, it could have been something the quarry men placed there. Perhaps a young apprentice was told to chip away until he made a perfect circle in the stone? All in all it is just another mystery that makes this wonderful area such a joy.

Please do make a journey to this area, there are many paths to follow and I can recommend that not only will you become aware of the power that Nature has to offer around here but you should become aware of the past mingling with the present as well. One day, whenever it is ready, the Earth will allow us to discover some more of the many and varied secrets that it protects around here. Hopefully.

2
SEVENTH CHILD OF A SEVENTH CHILD

I first met George Williamson a number of years ago just after one of my books had been published. He had read it and wanted to tell me "a few things" he thought I should be aware of. I am forever grateful.

Then, just after New Year in 1995, I received a telephone call from him; he had just finished reading my book on Staffordshire and wanted to talk to me. He could, he said, fill me in with one or two things, so round I went to his cosy terraced cottage home in Macclesfield. It is always a delight to talk to George for we are interested in the same thing - we are on the same wavelength as it were. He is now in his eighties but looks more like he's in his sixties and certainly has a very enquiring mind and a retentive memory. He has, in his time, been a highly skilled silk weaver (it runs in the family, both his parents and grandparents followed the skill) and up until recently he was demonstrating the art of silk weaving on looms to visitors at the working silk museum, Paradise Mill, in the town.

George had spent a number of years before and after the second world war living close to the Bridestones at the back of the Cloud. He met and married his first wife Dorothy "Dolly" Moss, a local lass, and they lived at Overton Hall. Consequently he had a good number of anecdotes to tell me about that area and the people who resided there. First and foremost he put me right about one point - I had referred to the pagan stone, now Christianised and known as Shepherd's Cross, as being on Biddulph Moor *(Staffordshire: Its Magic and Mystery)* but, he said, it is in fact on Biddulph Park. I am happy to make that clear - thank you, George!

He referred to the fact that my Great Aunt, Hannah Pickford, had been a Wise Woman and practised her art at her home, Hannah's Buildings, on the Roaches; she was the sort of person who could heal almost anything.

"My missus had an aunt who was just the same," he told me. "She was a Wise Woman up on Cloudside before the second world war," he said and, as we both drank a very welcome cup of tea, he went on to explain about his wife's aunty and much, much more.

But first of all he had something to tell me about his dear departed first wife (he is now very happily married to his third). "She had the Gift of Fay" he said to me. I thought I knew what he meant but felt it best to ask him to elaborate.

"She was a Fay Woman - she had Second Sight; people used to say she had Second Sight." He explained: "She knew what was going to happen before it did."

He finished off his cup of tea and placed it down on the polished table. "It's not surprising and no one up at the Cloud thought anything of it; after all she was the seventh child of a seventh child. And she was born on the Sabbath." (It is more usual for the Seventh Son of a Seventh Son to be credited with the gift of Second Sight but I have subsequently been told that, although this is the generality, in the border country of Staffordshire and Cheshire either male or female children who were the seventh child of a seventh child received this accolade. They were expected to use their gift for the good of the community in general and really had no option but to look into the future of their friends and neighbours just as soon as they were old enough and able enough).

In point of fact, his wife did not relish this gift. She was, there is no doubt, extremely talented but she was also, according to George, rather uncertain of the powers she had. He confided she was not entirely pleased at being 'blessed' with the gift and was rather frightened of the powers she possessed, although she would not have told a soul (apart from her husband) of her fears.

So what did George mean by 'The Gift of Fay'? He was using a phrase common in the hills and valleys around the Staffordshire, Derbyshire and Cheshire borders that was used to explain someone who not only had the gift of prophesy and Second Sight (the Third Eye) but who had other gifts that mere mortals were not blessed with. For this was, and still is, the Land of Mystery. I firmly believe this area is the place where one of the earliest traditions of the people of the Faery, the Fae people, originated. Their traditions lived on in the legends of a strange race of dark-skinned people with small features who were said to be descendants of the Saracens and who lived on Biddulph Moor. I have laboured long and hard on my theories into this in a book on Staffordshire and would here merely point out that one of the most common surnames in the area used to be 'Fay'. It is now a common belief that perhaps the Fae People were the first in this land, the Little Dark People or the Picts, the Old Ones; *Robin Hood, Green Lord of the Wildwood,* John Matthews, Gothic Image Publications 1993. The name 'Fay' is thought to come from the Latin 'fata' describing the personal fates befalling men. The Fata were supernatural females who paid visits to the cots of new-born babes. 'Fay' became the word for enchanted or bewitched and 'fay-erie' signified an enchanted land. The two became intermingled and 'fays' became 'fairies' in most areas but retained its original meaning in the Land of the Three Shires, particularly around Leek, Macclesfield and Congleton.

But let's return to George's tale as he told me over the cup, or two, of tea. He mentioned a number of instances when his wife was able to tell the future and these were times when people had not actually asked what was in store. She would meet someone and know, instantly, what fate was to befall them. This could be a great responsibility and one that she knew could not be taken lightly. She did not want it, she had not asked for it, but people expected it of her. She did her very best to ignore it but it was with her constantly.

There is much that George knows about the area around the Cloud. He lived at Overton Hall (SJ 897 606) and there has long been a legend that there is a tunnel from there to Biddulph Old Hall (SJ 894 618). In the cellar of Overton Hall there is a bricked up archway, supposedly the start of this tunnel. George's first wife, Dolly, and their daughter have seen it and George once asked the present owners why they would not knock it down to see where the tunnel went. He was told in no uncertain terms that they would not because they did not know what would be found. It's as straightforward as that. George had heard that Overton Hall was once tenanted by two brothers who terrorised the area. They had taken the tenancy shortly after, he believed, the Battle of Waterloo and were rogues and vagabonds and everyone lived in fear of them. They also inhabited Crossley Hall near North Rode and were in cohoots with a local publican (he thinks Catstones House was once a public house and this could have been the place) and this publican was a 'fence' who took all the items they had stolen from the neighbourhood. These were the days when criminals could escape the law by going over the border, just as the Flash coiners are said to have done at Three Shires Head. Anyway, it appears the law eventually caught up with them and they were hanged at Stafford - so we can assume they were captured within the Staffordshire boundaries.

Higher Overton Farm is also reputed to have an underground tunnel from a cellar room that no-one has been able to discover. I firmly believe that these legends of underground tunnels from one ancient site to another are connected with earth energy lines. I think that these ancient buildings were deliberately placed upon these lines of force just as older sites, such as The Bridestones, were also built upon them. There is certainly an earth energy line running between Biddulph Old Hall and Overton Hall and the Bridestones site is not only placed firmly on an extremely powerful line but forms one corner of a triangle of ancient sites. We shall explore this later, as, for now, there is still much to keep us with George's recollections.

I chatted to George about the many carvings that have been made on the Cloud itself. Some, we agreed, are quite modern, and some I have drawn attention to before. There is one that looks quite old (although I am no geologist and cannot say for certain with the aid of anything scientific) that looks for all the world like a flying saucer. It may not be, of course, but take a look at it for yourself and please tell me what you make of it. I have tried to date it with the aid of a pendulum and have been given the date 1604 - perhaps other dowsers may like to have a go - it is on the

A carving on Bosley Cloud - is it of a flying saucer?

33

main rock face underneath the 'trig' point and slightly to the north. There are others like the carved head - perhaps something to do with the Celtic Cult of the Head - and there is one that looks like a deer or bison. Another appears to represent the Double Sunset of which Bosley Cloud is very much a part (*Magic, Myth and Memory*). Yet another shows what could very well be the 'tree of life'. George told me that he recalled his aunt's farm at Cloudside and there, placed on a wall, were two carved blocks of stone in the shape of heads. One was like a gargoyle with an open mouth, he said, and he had been told that they had been carved by stonemasons and given to his Aunt Harriet who lived at the Cloudside Farm.

It was then that we began to compare our Aunts! I had a Great Aunt Hannah who was a Healer, a Wise Woman - the person who would be called upon to deliver a baby, tend a wound or heal a broken bone - and George's Aunt Harriet (in fact his wife's aunt) from Cloudside was the same sort of person. She had once healed the broken bone of a mason and it is thought those carved heads had been carved for her in payment. The last time George returned there, in 1966, they had gone. It was this same Aunt Harriet whose niece was a Fay Woman but did not want The Gift. Perhaps proof that this talent is inherited through our genes.

Sacrifices from the rock

There was a great deal more in store for me from George's memory banks and we settled down to yet another cup of tea as we sat around the dining room table that was laid out with old maps of the area. He began to recall one of the many characters who used to live there (every rural area spawned these characters at one time and we are poorer for their rarity now). He described the man as a high-class tramp who was affectionately known as 'Cap'. No doubt some other mature Cloudsiders may recall knowledge of him.

'Cap' knew everyone in the area and he knew the people who used to travel through - the sellers of merchandise, the cattle dealers, the Romanies and many more. These were the people who knew the area better than many who had lived there all their lives for these travellers' parents, grandparents and who knows who had been passing through that land for countless centuries and they had known almost everyone who had resided there. In consequence they know the tales - the legends, the traditions, the fears and the superstitions. 'Cap' was a mine of information. He knew everyone or he knew someone who did. He was that sort. No-one really knew where he came from or where he went, he just seemed to be there. And the tales he told were legion. So many, in fact, that George could not recount one half of them. 'Cap' had his own version of the history of the area and he swore it was the true version. Who are we to argue? He related that the historians would have it that the Romans once built a camp at Hulme Walfield to contain the renegade British but he knew the spot to be Tall Ash at Buglawton, within sight of the Cloud.

But the favourite tale he would tell was of the Catstones or Cat Stones. These stones (SJ 897 636) are at the back of the plantation atop the Cloud and form the stunning backdrop to Catstones House, a delightful and stately abode. These tall rocks form a sheer face some fifty feet or more in height and have a flat top. This was the place, said 'Cap', where sacrifices were made to the cat goddess. This temple of the cat worshippers was the place where sacrificial victims were thrown down the rock face to die on the altar at the bottom. This, he confidently stated, took place at the spring equinox - the pagan time of rebirth that was taken over by the Christian church and became Easter.

Up until very recently, during every Good Friday, thousands upon thousands of people from Congleton and Macclesfield and the surrounding areas would journey to the Cloud - a throwback, he maintained, to the time when these sacrifices were made.

Our friend 'Cap' was not the only one to believe this. I have heard it from other sources and perhaps this could be the origin of the Cheshire Cat? If so, the carved stone head depicting the grinning cat at Pott Shrigley Church - by the side of the altar - is a pagan throwback to the Old Ways, and if so the memory of worshipping the goddess Cattha has, unwittingly, been carried on.

There is also the tradition that the Catstones form the shape of a cat. In early February of 1995 Maurice Winnell and I decided to have a close look at this rock face. The owners of Catstones House readily gave us the go ahead to walk over their property to come face to face with the Cat and this we did one lunch time. They were out when we called but their gardener was burning cuttings from the rhododendron bushes at the rear. Seeing two unlikely looking characters with dowsing rods, maps and cameras in hand he thought he had better check what they were up to, but on satisfying himself that we were harmless but perhaps a little 'eccentric' we got into conversation. He was a local chap and had heard the legends concerning the Stones and knew there was supposed to be a cat depicted in them but had never really looked closely. Isn't it always the case? Whatever is on your own doorstep is so often taken for granted. We examined the rock face carefully and every crack and curve began to look, to us, like a cat.

Some weeks earlier we had been on the top of the Cloud in the plantation in driving rain and swirling mist. We were examining a tumulus - a Neolithic burial ground - more or less above the Catstones and were using the dowsing rods. A lady came out of the mist. She was walking her dog along the footpath and as she set eyes on us was a little unsure about just what was going on - and who could have blamed her! However, Maurice got into conversation with her and told her we were dowsing a tumulus - an ordinary everyday activity for us - and she seemed at ease.

"I've got a friend who knows someone who writes about that sort of thing," the lady told Maurice. "Her name is Linda Skellam and she is a Healer - a reflexologist. This friend of hers writes about dowsing and ley lines in this area". She was referring to yours truly and I introduced myself. We talked about the Catstones and how she - who was a next door neighbour to the owners of Catstones House - had clearly seen the outline of a cat in the rocks.

Our subsequent visit to Catstones House and our conversation with the gardener coincided with his burning the cuttings, as I have mentioned. Unfortunately for us he had placed his bonfire directly in front of the supposed sacrificial stone - and the smoke was intense. The wind swirled the smoke about and our attempts to identify the cat proved difficult. We did think we had seen an outline and then a different outline took shape in our imaginations and then another. So that was it - or so we thought. On returning to our car parked in the road we glanced back at the enigmatic rock face and there, as plain as plain could be, was the shape of a cat clearly defined in the rock face. We walked another foot or two and the shape disappeared and it then only became definable again because the sun was casting its shadows at a certain angle. The cat's face comes and the cat's face goes. Now you see it, now you don't. Surely a magical and mysterious sign to the worshippers of the cat goddess?

There is much more to come to light around this area and we could linger for a great deal longer. Before we take a look at the enigmatic Bridestones Triangle we should, I think, glance at just one more building around Bosley Cloud or the Cloud. It is called Big Fenton Farm. Black and white half timbered, it is in a delightful setting. Legend has it that it was being carried through the sky by angels in search of a suitable spot for it and they were frightened by the dark and jagged edges of Bosley Cloud and released their burden. As it fell to the ground on the crest of a small hill in the valley below the Cloud the force of the impact caused the earth in front to split open but the angels beautified the scar by filling it with water so that their lovely building could look at its own image in the silver mirror. It was then named Big Fenton - Fent meaning a split.

What is for certain is that this building has been there since the 17th century and the Cheshire historian and romantic novelist Beatrice Tunstall used it as part of her setting for a novel "The Dark Lady" about the Fyttons of Gawsworth. In her book, its name was Silverpit.

I have come across Beatrice before. She knew a lot about Cheshire traditions and another of her novels, "The Shiny Night" took me in search of a witch's house at Bunbury. It was as a result of this that I received a charming note and some press cuttings from Myra Ross of Macclesfield Road, Prestbury. In her letter she mentioned the book by Beatrice Tunstall and told me that on page 101 the right of way through 'Silverpit' was mentioned and also a mound visible as the traveller comes out of the right of way which is supposed to be a burial mound and harbours the ghost of the Grey Lady. A burial mound or tumulus such as this was often associated with a ghost and sometimes was referred to as a Fairy Mound. This was a place where no farmer would plough and no feet would tread and perhaps goes a little way to explaining why so many of these mounds, some as old as 4000 years, are still (thankfully) with us.

(At the time of writing this I have just returned from a visit to a field near to Sandbach. I received a communication from a white witch - a gentleman in his 80s - who told me about this piece of land known locally as a Fairy Field and he extended an invitation for me to visit. The first thing I saw as I clambered over the stile into the field was a tumulus.)

But to return to Big Fenton Farm: It is said that at one time a public footpath went directly through the farmhouse and one of the front wings used to be used as a chapel. On one side of the chapel there was a wooden structure, very much like a pen, and on this was a large bloodstain, said to have been there for centuries, although no-one has satisfactorily been able to describe its origin. Did this pen contain someone who was injured, and therefore bleeding, and was in need of spiritual and physical healing at the chapel? Perhaps. Or, then again, there is the tale that there used to be sacrifices made at this place a very long time ago. Has this anything at all to do with the nearby Catstones, I wonder? Have

Big Fenton Farm - carried through the air by angels according to an old adage. It is also the site of hauntings and other strange events. *Congleton Chronicle*

remnants of the traditions of sacrifices being made survived in the telling of the tales about this building? Who knows! This has proven to be the case at other places at other times and the entire area around the Cloud is so alive with magic, myth and legend that it could very well be the case.

Beatrice Tunstall was a very spiritual lady and she had the

The Catstones. If you look carefully then the outline of a cat will be noticeable to some. Others look long and hard and never see. Was the goddess Catha or Catta worshipped here and sacrifices made to her?

eye for seeing what was there and what was hidden away. She often wrote in an enigmatic manner and much of what she said is hidden within her words. A sad reflection on those pre-war days when anything that did not conform with established ideas was looked upon as 'odd'.

The Bridestones Triangle

I hope I've already whetted your appetite with a couple of references to what I have termed The Bridestones Triangle. Now it is my duty to explain.

Some of you will be familiar with the way I and others usually attempt to track ley lines, earth energy lines or whatever is the popular term for them at the moment. Quite simply: divining rods are used. Nothing elaborate and quite often just a couple of bent wire coat hangers although some people I know are advanced enough to use nothing but their bare hands to pick up and define these energy flows that are within the earth's crust. I have not been a great believer in just getting a map and drawing a straight line between ancient sites and then calling it a ley line for I have always liked to get out in the field, as it were, and see for myself whether or not this undefinable energy does actually flow within the earth along this particular line or another. Don't get me wrong, I'm not knocking that particular form of following the Old Straight Tracks, it just has not appealed to me and I do know that some extremely strong lines have been discovered that way.

However, on a particularly frosty February morning I opened a large brown envelope delivered by the postman. It contained a 14-page document, printed on both sides, entitled *Gateway to Infinity, a Study of Circular Ley Patterns in England* David R. Furlong Ibis Press, 51 Rodney Road, Cheltenham. I knew nothing about Mr Furlong or his study and there was nothing else in the envelope - but on the back was one of those black and gold stickers containing someone's name and address. It read 'Marjorie Kola' with an address in Stockport and, likewise, I knew nothing about Marjorie.

I read the study's introduction and was pleased to note that it was written by someone who, like me, liked to experience the ley lines for themselves. David was not a dowser but he sensed certain spots as "having an atmosphere". So instead of drawing pencil line after pencil line on Ordnance Survey maps he went out and about and only registered points he knew possessed an 'atmosphere'. From this he discovered ley lines but developed his study to the extent that he discovered evidence for circular ley lines. I had not directly come across this theory before and found it extremely interesting and devoured the sometimes very technical information contained therein.

But who was Marjorie Kola and why had she sent this to me? I telephoned her and explained who I was and why I was phoning and thanked her for sending me the paper. It transpired that we had, in fact, met some three or four years before when I gave a talk to the Friends of Aquarius at Wilmslow - but her name was not then 'Marjorie Kola'. It was something much more mundane and she had changed it on the advice of a person she described as a Shaman. He had told her the name would react much better for her and so, without hesitation she changed it. She told me she had never looked back since then - wonderful things were always happening to her! She remembered my talk and thought I would be interested in reading the study on circular ley lines and had placed it in a drawer. A few years later she came across it and promptly posted it to me. It was worth waiting for.

Anyway, this study involved not only circular patterns but pyramid shapes. I have mentioned in my Peak District book about the famous triangle made up of the Bull Ring at Dove Holes, Arbor Low and Wet Withers stone circle on Eyam Moor - these ancient sites form the three corners of a perfect triangle - a fact discovered, or re-discovered, some while ago by people much more worthy than I, and I wondered whether there was anything similar within our Land of the Three Shires.

Where to start was not too difficult. I took hold of an Ordnance Survey Map SJ 86/96 I knew contained the Bridestones and took it from there. An 'X' marked the spot, in pencil, for the Bridestones - those enigmatic remains of a once proud structure of many stones looking westward towards Ireland, the home of the builders of that stone temple.

What else was there? A straight line running eastwards crossed Axstone Spring at Heaton. Up until quite recently there was a stone within this vicinity known as the Ax Stone and I recall being taken to it by a great friend by the name of Geoff Browne who used to live in Leek. At the time of writing he is the editor of a Classic Cars magazine and being paid for indulging in his devouring passion of old cars, lucky man! I then recalled how Geoff had shown me the stone and mentioned it lined up with the Bridestones and was also on a powerful line that extended to Snowdon in the west and Stonehenge in the south. If the Axstone is still there then I have been unable to find it - I fear it has been removed by someone with no ill intent but merely out of ignorance of what it really was, but the spring is still a prominent landmark.

Further east and the line came to the Roaches although there are so many powerful rocks within this Land of the High Rocks that choosing any one in particular would be difficult, I thought. But then logic ruled and I measured the exact distance between the Bridestones and Axstone Spring and extended it eastwards. This took the line to the boundaries of Roach House and to the region of the Bawd Stone, that healing rock perched on three smaller stones and mentioned by me on many previous occasions.

Assuming that this line was the base of any possible triangle, then Axstone Spring should be in the centre of that line. Drawing along the edge of a ruler directly north the pencil mark stopped when it came to Cluelow Cross just north of Wincle. Cluelow Cross is an ancient stone pillar atop an artificial mound some 250 feet in diameter and 25 feet high. It has been said, not least by Dr Sainter in his Victorian work *Scientific Ramblings Around Macclesfield* that the cross was erected not simply as a marker but as a pointer to what was underneath.

So there we have it. A triangle. I don't want to get too technical - not least because mathematical mysteries have never been my strong point, but do check it out. The two base corners are each 48 degrees and the apex corresponds. There has been much written about the sacred triangles and relationships with the Great Pyramids (although we have a natural pyramid on our own doorsteps - the lofty Shutlingslow) and I would recommend John Mitchell's now classic work *View Over Atlantis* if you wish to pursue this further.

And of course, because our triangle is split down the middle by the line from Cluelow Cross to Ax Spring it makes two triangles, in fact. You pays your money and you takes your choice, as the saying goes! It may, of course, be that these triangular measurements are a pure coincidence but I will let you judge that for yourself. If they are then they are an amazing coincidence. Roach House, close by the Bawdstone, on the easterly corner of the triangle is an extremely old building and I have heard it said within my family (who lived on the Roaches for many centuries) that it was built by the site of a building once used as a church or place of religious gatherings. If this is the case then it is perhaps possible that the religious building was placed there for a very good reason as was so often the case with Christian structures - they were erected on a site used by earth worshippers - pagans. Just before we leave this area around Bosley Cloud and the

Bridestones, I have a footnote to a strange case I once told the world about.

Readers of my previous works may recall I mentioned the odd instance of the businessman who was 'abducted' after he had stopped his car by the Bridestones. He saw a strange light shining above the ancient stones and the next thing he knew he was in a copse some way down the road and he had lost two or three hours. I have never referred to this as a possible UFO abduction and neither has he (in point of fact he wants nothing at all to do with it any more) but some eminent UFOlogists have been pursuing the story.

I have been told that if a car parks outside Bridestones House (the building nearby named after the ancient stones) and switches on its headlights the stones become illuminated and that is, perhaps, what he saw as he stood by his parked car on the roadway. Secondly, there is a strong local tradition that the Bridestones affect both people and animals. Locals always used to break into a run if they happened to be passing by the stones because, they feared, their power affected people. Very often animals would be 'spooked' if they went by. I understand that in the 1950's a local farmer was riding a horse along there and the horse, on passing the Bridestones, panicked and jumped a drystone wall towards Gooseberry (or Goseberry) Lane. The farmer fell off and was, unfortunately, killed. Dogs have been known to go mad in that vicinity and George Williamson told me that whenever he and his wife used to walk by them they would break into a run. "Neither of us ever felt safe there" he said. Could the same have been experienced by the business man who had such a strange 'encounter' right there?

And I have been informed that some years ago some people called at Bridestones House and asked if they could hold a "service" at the Bridestones. They explained that there was an evil presence at the

Stones and they wished to rid it. There is public access to the site and they could have gone there without seeking permission but nevertheless, agreeably, did ask. They performed their rituals around a fire and at the conclusion were happy that the task they set out to perform had been completed.

Perhaps they laid to rest the soul of the lady whose bones had originally been buried in the Bridestones Chamber? Her bones were obviously not allowed to rest in peace because at some time they had been removed. Perhaps she had been a sacrifice or

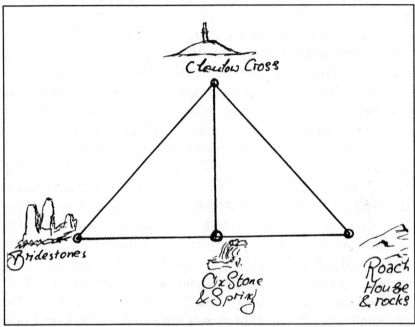

The Bridestones Triangle with Cluelow Cross, Axstone, and the Roaches, around the Bawdstone and Roach House. Is it just a pure coincidence that the ancient sites are set out this way? Some have made lengthy studies of the layout of sites such as this and can find geometric designs in the positioning of old churches within cities, for instance. This takes us on to the secrets of the masons and their Ancient Knowledge. Was this knowledge passed down to them from those who planned the Bridestones Triangle? On a much bigger scale it is possible to connect Stonehenge and Avebury and Arbor Lowe but if this is done then it should be noted that several points within our Three Shires - the Bridestones especially - fall within this 'sacred geography'.

perhaps the Bridestones were erected for her. We shall probably never know, although a number of psychics have put forward what they have found at the spot and most have come to similar conclusions - whoever was placed there was a person who was worshipped by those who buried her.

That tells us but little, for often sacrificial victims were special people who were sacrificed precisely because they were special - the Divine Victims. However, one psychic I know has visited the spot and saw that the lady buried there had been interred after a ritual ceremony during which she was garrotted and then her body was mummified and worshipped for 'two seasons' before being placed in the chamber. She wore a gold band round her head and her robes were of rich red.

The act of garrotting has oftimes been referred to as the "Cheshire Smile" - the neck being cut from ear to ear. We have already come across that in this book. And I'm sure it will rear its head again. Looking over the Cheshire Plain from the Bridestones it would be possible (if the trees were not in the way!) to see Lindow Common and more precisely Lindow Pool where the preserved body of 'Lindow Man' or 'Pete Marsh' was discovered. He was a Divine Victim - a sacrifice. He, too, was garrotted.

Missionaries visit the Heathens

Another religious building was erected on the Roaches because of the heathen aspect of the folks who lived around there. It was called Newstone Chapel, part of the Leek Methodist Circuit, and was placed against the easterly end of Newstone Farm. The fact that the Methodist Elders thought it necessary to send 'missionaries' to the natives of those High Rocks is interesting in itself but, more to the point, why did they choose Newstone? Its very name implies that if there was a 'new' stone there could have been an 'old' stone. And when a rock or stone is referred to as 'old' the implication is that it has been an object of renown - something to be worshipped, or where worship took place - or, at the very least, where traditions are set. Was the 'Old' Stone toppled or destroyed at some time and replaced by the 'New' Stone? I certainly think so and know I am not alone with that assumption. There is an interesting rock formation there, a 'rocking' stone, that may have found its way there quite naturally, or then again it may have been placed there. It resembles the stone at Ballstone Farm close by and here the god Baal was worshipped and the Beltane Fires lit. The Beltane Fires were lit all around the Roaches up until the nineteenth century and there are tales of them still going to this day. Mind you, there are a great many secrets still kept up on the Roaches and some of them will never be told.

The Beltane fires were lit on the eve of May 1st - the same time when people used to process to the Bawdstone for healing purposes - and perhaps, and only perhaps, if you were to journey there at that time of year you just may witness a fire or two at certain spots. These fires were cleansing fires, and livestock (and people) would pass through them to be cleansed. They were an amazing site at one time, I would imagine. The whole land would be ablaze on May 1st but that tradition has all but died, or has been murdered.

There are still people who live on the Roaches who would refer to themselves as, if not earth worshippers, then certainly believers in the powers of the earth. I class many of them as very good friends and although I no longer live on the Roaches myself, I can often be found there. As the religious piece says: "I will lift up mine eyes to the hills, from whence cometh my help." If ever you find yourself in need of spiritual upliftment then please make a pilgrimage to these rocks. There is evidence that the Celts, the Danes and the Normans all found these High Rocks a place of power. Do, please, try them for what they can give and I am sure

Newstone - does its name imply it replaced an 'Old' stone that was the centre of local 'knowledge'?

you will find your own god there.

Much has been written about these High Rocks and much more will be written in the future. A lot of recent interest has centred on the strange building known as Rock Hall or Rock Hall Cottage, mainly because of a larger than life character named Douglas Moller who used to live there along with his wife, Anne. Although they came to the area from Liverpool they carry a similar appendage to the name Mellor which is one of the local names for this region. At one time there were but a few families resident on the Roaches. One was Mellor, another was Bowyer, Pickford was another and there was also Sweatmore and Gould. There were others, but these were the main ones.

Douglas and his wife took up residence at this strange dwelling built into the rocks and, indeed, partly constructed around some of the rocks that had fallen thereabouts and very soon he became quite 'notorious' as a character. His eye patch and wild hair added to the mystique of the man who was soon dubbed 'Lord

49

of the Roaches'. He fought a campaign against the Peak Park who wanted him out of the cottage and eventually the couple did move out but not before a lengthy battle was fought.

Lord Doug bought the place for £6000 and it had been empty for many years before he moved in. It had suffered both the ravages of time and vandals and squatters had also claimed it. Back in 1861 Sir Philip Brocklehurst of Swythamley Hall placed his gamekeeper there, for there is a magnificent view from its windows and he would have been able to keep a good eye out on the land. These windows are placed rather oddly at first glance but a look through them from the inside shows that they were put where they are to command a panoramic view.

But this cottage was occupied way before Sir Philip's gamekeeper took up residence there. One of its most famous residents was the legendary Bess Bower or Bowyer and some of her descendants live not only on the Roaches but in Leek and Macclesfield as well to this day. I have the pleasure of knowing a number of them. It certainly seems to have attracted 'characters' but perhaps that has all gone now because the Peak Park have made it a climbing centre. We shall have to see.

Bess Bowyer lived at Rock Hall for a good number of years in the nineteenth century and a great amount of research has been conducted into her and the rest of the Bowyer 'clan' by Mr Colin Bowyer who lives in Leek. The legendary Bess was born on the Roaches around the year 1785 and had three children but never married in the eyes of the church. This was not uncommon then - some people used to get married 'over the brush' by walking to the Bridestones and the man and woman walking around the stones.

Perhaps this has some connection with Brigit, the fertility goddess who gave her name to these stones. Others travelled to the Bull Ring at Dove Holes and, no doubt, there were other sacred spots now lost to our knowledge. Marriage like this was, of course, frowned upon by the Church but more often than not in isolated areas like here the authorities were unaware and, anyway, most could not afford to pay for a church wedding in those days.

Bess's children were John Robinson Bowyer born around 1815, Hannah Bowyer born 1825 and Eliza Bowyer born 1831. Eliza died at the age of five and is buried at Leek. Hannah probably was nicknamed Doxey and lived with her mother in the cave-cum-cottage that is now Rock Hall and they managed to eke out a living of sorts by making besoms which were sold at nearby markets like Buxton, Leek and Macclesfield. When Hannah was somewhere around 20 years of age she gave birth to David. He, too, was illegitimate and then some time later she disappeared, leaving her son at Rock Hall. It is thought by Mr Bowyer that Hannah was either abducted by an Irish vagrant or she left with one by her own free will. This area had many visits from these Irish travellers at the time and many passed through after embarking at Liverpool and journeying to the East Midlands. They were, in the main, fleeing the potato famine. Interestingly, this is not the only Irish connection with local familes - more later.

There is no doubt that Bess and her family were extremely poor and it is recorded they had been given a dole of bread by the Leek Poor Law Guardians in 1846. Bess also received a pair of shoes from them. She died at the age of 75 and was buried at Meerbrook. There is another local tradition concerning Bess and that is that she divided the cave into two parts, one for the night and one for the day, and through both flowed an ice cold stream of water. In her bedroom was a secret door that led to the rocky crags at the back of the building through which she assisted smugglers and deserters to escape from the militia who went to bring them back. Bess, according to tradition, was descended from 'Bowyer of the Rocks' a 'moss trooper' or freebooter. Perhaps Bowyer of the Rocks had something to do with the notorious Flash coiners who operated hereabouts.

Nearby is Doxey Pool, a 'flash' or dew pond or, indeed, just a pool that stands on Hen Cloud. Close to this was, at one time, Doxey Cottage and, as I have mentioned in other publications, the word Doxey could mean many things, one of which implies a lady of easy morals. So where did Hannah's nickname come from? Was it from the same source that gave its name to the nearby pool and cottage or not? I'll leave you to be the judge. This pool does, of course, carry with it a tradition of a mere maid residing within but legends of the Roaches are as common as the bilberries up there!

There has been a tradition, carried on by 'Lord Doug', that a flat stone slab that forms part of the roof of Rock Hall or Cottage was once used for human sacrifices. Another says that there was once a twelve hour battle fought there between two men over land and a lady. After it became obvious that neither could win the fight they agreed to divide the land but the lady in question was so upset that she would have nothing to do with them from then onwards. Just above the building on the rocks where many a climber has learned the ropes, so to speak, is a stone carved into a sort of chair. Many people have conjectured what this could be but many are also aware that it was carved specifically for a Royal visit. I was once told that the stone chair was much older than thought at one time and was merely utilised during the visit of 1872. But not so, I'm afraid because I know for an absolute fact that it was carved by my great great grandfather, Isaac Pickford, assisted by his son William. The occasion was the summer of 1872 when the Roaches were visited by Prince and Princess Teck and the Swythamley Squire Brocklehurst entertained the royal party to a picnic there. The event was marked by a fir tree being planted at the entrance to the cave by Princess Mary of Cambridge.

Perhaps we should here return to the 'Irish connection'. One of the great sorrows of my life is that I did not listen more closely to some of those things I was told by both my father and grandfather. They both knew this area intimately. Anyway, one of the things I do recall is my father saying there was Irish blood within the family. All well and good, because there must be few families indeed that cannot boast some Celtic connection along the way. However, a look at the family tree that goes back a good number of centuries gives no indication whatsoever that this was

Rock Hall or Cottage as it is today - now a climbing centre.

53

correct. So where did he get the idea from? Most families upon the Roaches have recollections of visits made, on a regular basis, by Irish 'travellers' - not the people we refer to today as 'travellers' but folk who would visit on a regular basis. They usually put in an appearance at lambing time or during the harvesting and they were all known extremely well indeed by the families they visited. So much so that they were 'a part of the family', as it were. And their fathers, grandfathers and great grandfathers had visited at regular intervals as well. They were part and parcel of life up there. But why the Roaches? I think because their roots could, possibly, be traced back to the times when the Celts were rulers of that domain. Let me explain a little further. I have mentioned the Flash coiners often enough before. Tradition has it that they comprised travellers, hawkers or tinkers who passed counterfeit coins and escaped conviction by hopping from shire to shire at Three Shires Head. These were people firmly established in the area during the early 1700s and were, in all probability, of Irish stock.

My very good friend Frank Parker of Ballstone Farm has a theory. It concerns the entire area being a Celtic enclave at one time and this area was led by a Chief, or Leader. The Irish for such a person is phonetically pronounced 'Teeshot' - the same as the leader of the Eire Government today. And now we come to the 'Teapot Club'. Again, I have mentioned this before, but briefly it was a society supposedly set up by local people regularly saving in a large teapot and if ever anyone needed the money for illness or a funeral the cash was emptied and the savings started again until the next time there was a need. Unfortunately, the Flash Loyal Union or 'Teapot Club' came to a halt in the early 1990s. However, as quaint as this story is, there is something slightly amiss - where is the teapot so cherished by the club? No one has ever known, it would appear. At least not within living memory. And further, why a teapot? Surely tea was a very rare and costly commodity when the

Teapot Club was formed? Could the once familiar sound of 'Teeshot' have become 'Teapot'? Was this Club a remnant of the Celtic past and were the visitors from across the sea another connection with the Celtic past? Frank has other theories but it would be wrong of me to steal his glory. Perhaps one day he will put them into print. Here's hoping.

There are countless mysteries upon the Roaches. It is that sort of place. Look up at them from Meerbook or Upperhulme and they are magnificent in their splendour. They are cold and domineering and they are welcoming. A contradiction in terms but go and see what I mean. Look down at them from the old ridgeway that passes the Mermaid Inn and they do not look all that powerful. True, the scenery is magnificent but they could hardly be classed as mountains, merely a hilly and rocky range. It is the magic within that is so important. It is a magic that is very much alive and it is a very powerful magic indeed. There is nothing sinister about it. It is entirely natural. Pay a visit on a summer's day and the area is thronged with trippers. Nothing wrong in that, for they are as entitled to enjoy and appreciate the area as much as anyone. I hope they go there for the right reasons. But, for me, the time to visit is when the mountain mist blankets the rocks, when the curlew calls to its hidden mate and the shadows cast spells and hide secrets. Another favourite time is when the wind is howling like a banshee forcing the sheep to huddle against the drystone walls and the birds shelter in the clefts. Few are about then and it is at these times that the spirits of people past come alive and the rocks themselves welcome you. It is a time when you can walk the old tracks and clamber over the old paths along with the Watchers. They are all around. I and Hilary have met my ancestors and have been told things we did not know when we have been on those mystic stones. You can, also. Just try it.

The royal chair carved out of rock. There are a number of legends, or myths, surrounding this chair. It is supposed to have been used by a 'wild man' who lived in the vicinity. Anyway, the views from it will knock your socks off!

Another mystery of the Roaches. This stone has an eye carved in it and looks like a serpent, hence its name 'The Serpent Stone'. Who carved the eye, and why? If you were to look from the nearby Bawdstone to where the Spring Solstice can be seen then the Serpent Stone marks the spot. Perhaps it is a reference to the Dragon, Snake or Serpent - names given to Earth Energy?

3
IN SEARCH OF THE EARTH GODDESS

'Seek and Ye Shall Find' say the scriptures, and if you search for the Earth Goddess, the Earth Mother or, as most of us tend to refer to her today 'Mother Earth' then she will cradle you in her arms. Like the Biblical Prodigal Son and the paternal figure welcoming him back to the fold, the maternal figure will also welcome the prodigals back to the fold.

I once had the pleasure of spending an idyllic Sunday in the woods at Alderley Edge with a group of people. We did nothing but wander the area. The sun was shining and it attracted half of Cheshire, or so it seemed, to that magical spot and we were no exception. The car park was heaving and Grannelli's ice cream van was doing a roaring trade. Most of those visiting on that glorious day were there to take in the atmosphere of the spot and to take in the beauty. They might not have known it but they were also either showing respect to Mother Earth or admiring (some would say worshipping) her. Our group strolled to the little known spots that are essentially what the Edge is really all about and we were communing with nature just like everyone else. We were doing exactly what has been done for many many centuries - and there's nothing wrong with it at all. It's harmless and it's enjoyable, uplifting, invigorating and very very healthy. We saw chaffinches, robins, coal tits and starlings and we enjoyed their songs and we enjoyed their antics. We were uplifted by the buds on the trees and looked forward to the impending summertime and we were enraptured by the sunbeams shining through the trees onto the earth below. As the squirrels leaped, so did our hearts. Corny perhaps and somewhat old fashioned to some but I would venture to suggest it is they who are missing so much. Perhaps these prodigals will, at some time, return to the fold also.

And as we passed the 'well' or spring where the water tinkles from the rocks and where centuries before the Celtic peoples worshipped at the womb of the Earth Mother we paused. Some paid their respects to her. Others just stood and soaked in the atmosphere or drank of her waters. This is known as the Healing Well and has nothing whatsoever to do with the one carved by the Victorians and known as the Wizard's Well. That is there to attract the tourists whereas the other 'well' used to attract pilgrims.

We still worship the Earth Mother in Derbyshire and Staffordshire every summer at the wells, especially in Derbyshire, and the curious aspect here is that it is not only condoned by the Christian church but positively encouraged. Whereas in the sixteenth and seventeenth centuries the church positively discouraged earth worship and destroyed many sanctuaries around these healing and life-giving waters it has now gone full circle and the sacred waters are once again festooned with finery and homage is paid. Now this is but one aspect of how the Earth Mother is still with us. She is also remembered by those who follow the Old Ways - and there are many within these Three Shires who do just that - some will admit to it and some won't - and there is much evidence that she was remembered in days gone by.

Some would have it that when the workmen or stone masons were given the task of carving figures for the churches that were built in Norman times the vast majority of them followed the ways of old and may have given lip service to Christianity but were, in fact, worshippers of the earth - quite literally, pagans. And given this task of chiselling out coats of arms and heads of bold knights they also placed here and there figures that were not quite what they first appeared to be. In many instances they would be downright rude figures but they had a slight disguise or a cloak of respectability or, like the Emperor's New Clothes, no-one dared to show their own knowledge of such things and in consequence ignored what they suspected these carvings to be. A number of Derbyshire churches, for instance, have carvings of faces with their tongues sticking out. These grotesques are certainly ill-mannered for we tell our children to this day not to stick their tongues out because it is rude to do so. What we might not be aware of is the act of doing so signifies the exposure of the male genitalia. Rude indeed.

Today it has become unfashionable to credit the foliate heads or the Green Man figures with earth worship but I would disagree - each to their own as they say! One study of them in 1978 by Kathleen Basford concluded that these heads with foliage springing from their mouths, ears and (sometimes) eyes far from being representative of re-birth and the triumph of life over death (as spring triumphs over winter each year) in fact depicted lost souls or wicked spirits. Perhaps. And the Green Man or Jack in the Green - the figure who leads the Knutsford May Day procession each year - was said in 1979 by Roy Judge to have only stretched back to the late eighteenth century. Perhaps.

But throughout Cheshire, Staffordshire and Derbyshire there are still remnants of these traditions of life over death and rebirth. Down at Abbotts Bromley the famous Horn Dance shows the Man in Green triumphing over death and over at Antrobus in Cheshire the Soul Gang still glorify fertility and re-birth. Part of their age-old ritual involves fertilisation of the Earth Mother. And at Castleton in Derbyshire the ceremony known as Garland Day when a man with his head bedecked in floral garlands rides his horse through the town has associations with the foliate heads and the Cult of the Head and nestles side by side with Earth worship going back at least to the time of the Celts. And who cannot say that the original Earth Spirit, later known in many areas as Robin, the Man in Green, does not still walk with us, side by side and hand in hand? I think he was with our group at Alderley Edge on that glorious sunny day.

At Gawsworth, a few miles out of Macclesfield, where Elizabethan fiction has been interwoven with not only present day superstition but latter-day fact, there is a figure carved by the side of the southern porch entrance. At first glance it looks rather the same as all the rest (there is a grotesque face with its tongue poking out at this site, incidentally) save for the fact that it has worn away more than the others. I think there is a reason for that which I will explain shortly. This enigmatic figure looks, at first glance, rather like a monkey in a rather uncomfortable pose but a closer look shows it is a bald, elderly creature, sometimes unkindly called a 'hag', with it's arms holding it's legs wide apart and exposing itself. And what is shown is rather exaggerated in size. This is not an unusual figure, for it can be found on a number of churches and Ronald Sheridan and Anne Ross in their book *Grotesques and Gargoyles,* Newton Abbott, 1975, say that this kind of representation is a pagan deity dear to the people which the church was unable to eradicate and so allowed it to live side by side with the objects of Christian orthodoxy.

The name given to this Hag creature is Sheela-na-Gig and some would have it that the image was carved to frighten away demons and, more often than not, the image is carved on porches just as at Gawsworth. To pass through the porch was to symbolically pass through the Yoni of the Goddess - the gateway to death and to the Womb of Regeneration.

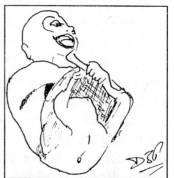

Look at this church and compare the other carvings. They do not seem to have been worn away so much as this Sheela-na-gig. They are all carved from the same kind of stone as well. I think that the figure has been worn

The Sheela-na-Gig at Gawsworth Church This ancient cult figure depicts the fertility aspects of the Old Religion and much more.

away by the very act of many hundreds if not thousands of hands touching it over the years as a ritual to encourage fertility. The hag is prominent in folklore and at nearby Swythamley on the edge of the moorland there is the legend of the old witch or hag who would transform herself into a hare. She lived at Hag Cottage. There are countless tales where the hare is important in folklore - often leading someone to either death or a long sleep. Merlin, for instance, was said to have been captured or imprisoned by Nimue disguised as a hare. The legend states he now guards the thirteen treasures of Britain and awaits rebirth. At Alderley Edge where the Merlin myths linger, the Shaman figure is said to be underground with thirteen knights waiting for England's hour of need. Close by is an area known as Hare Barrow. And in 1995 treasure was indeed found under the Edge - a hoard of Roman coins, hidden away for hundreds upon hundreds of years.

Just as the Earth Mother gives life, the Death Goddess is also depicted in our area. She was represented in long barrows or early ritual mounds thought to have been shaped like her body. She was both the possessor of a Womb and also a Tomb - see *The Ancient British Goddess,* Kathy Jones, Ariadne Publications, Somerset, 1991 and from which all souls would be hopefully re-born.

The fertility goddess Brigit is represented at the Bridestones on Bosley Cloud and at Mam Tor in Derbyshire, the hill upon which an ancient hill fort stands, was thought to be a breast of the goddess - part of the Sacred Landscape. According to Kathy Jones, in mythology Brigit is identified with Danu, Anu or Ana or later was said to be her daughter. The River Dane flows beneath the Bridestones and these waters are named after Danu. And on the Roaches in North Staffordshire is an area known as Ann Roach, the Rocks of Anu.

At Dove Holes, a small way out of Buxton, there still remains part of an ancient henge monument known as the Bull Ring. The stones have been removed - the last one in the 1700s, I believe - but it was still used up until recently by travellers - the true Romanies - as a meeting place and the spot where marriage ceremonies would take place. This certainly occurred during living memory for I spoke in 1995 to a lady in her late 50's who remembered witnessing a marriage ceremony there when she was a child.

Maurice Winnel and I dowsed the area of the Bull Ring at Doveholes and our dowsing rods informed us that there had been a total of 34 upright stones at the henge, at one time. There are no stones there now, save for the base of one just to the east of the northern entrance. The stones were about eight or nine feet apart.

4
THUNDER OF THE ANCIENTS

An ancient ley stone had stood, seemingly forever, above the roadway to Buxton from Macclesfield. It was in a field atop what is thought to be the site of an ancient burial. Certainly the mound it was placed upon stood proud of the earth, like a navel in the belly of the Mother. Today that old road to Buxton is still the most direct way from one ancient town to another but most motorists choose the Turnpike route - much more twisting and tortuous. And today that ancient stone stuck in the navel of Mother Earth is no longer with us.

When it was removed, however, the gods were angry and they showed it. In fact, they roared with anger - and it was not the only occasion that their voices were heard. This stone, some six feet in height, was one of very many that have dotted the landscape of the high lands of Derbyshire and Staffordshire - and to a lesser degree, Cheshire also. Many have been removed for whatever reason - during bouts of religious piety because they represented the Old Ways or just because they have got in the way of the plough. Why this particular stone was removed must be a matter of conjecture. The name given to this stone monolith was the Carne Stone, so-called because of a well known Macclesfield historian named May Carne who 'discovered' it. Perhaps she would have been the first to agree that she re-discovered it. May Carne passed over a few years ago and I, like so many, miss her greatly. She was a wonderful character who always reminded me of Margaret Rutherford in her finest roles as Miss Marple. She was the mainstay of the local historical society and she and I have had many a friendly argument over this, that or the other. She was not an orthodox historian, and perhaps that is why we both got on so well. She would not have the accepted view that history was a matter of dates. History was, for her, all about people. It was people who made history and always would, she once told me. Dates were of secondary importance. How right she was. I recall her putting forward a theory that the Royal and Ancient Borough of Macclesfield had at one point in its career been nothing more than a brothel for Roman soldiers. This did not go down too well, as you can imagine!

She did much work around the stone named after her. And during this time, on one particular afternoon in the early 70s, a violent thunderstorm occurred, raining the researchers off from their activities. Some while later, after an exhibition of photographs had been on display in the local library, including one of the Carne Stone, the mighty monolith was removed by the farmer who owned the field. Nothing illegal I would point out - but I and many others wish upon wish that it had been allowed to remain. However, as the stone was being removed another mighty thunderstorm broke out. Were the gods showing their anger?

This stone had been used as, among other things, a sight marker for many a weary traveller over those perilous and lonely moors for many a year. After the stone was removed a writer in the local paper said: 'Disrupting traffic signs now might bring a strong reaction from the long arm of the law but it would seem that the ancient inhabitants of this part of the world might have had more spectacular powers at their disposal. And just think what the penalty might have been for speeding!'

May Carne gave a series of six talks at the Macclesfield Teachers' Centre between 1974 and 1977 and one of them was entitled 'Macclesfield in Pre-History'. Thanks to Alina Burton and the good offices of the Historical Society I can quote from one part: Mrs Carne said, regarding the Carne Stone, that it used to stand in a field off Old Buxton Road. From New Buxton Road (now the main road) it could be quite clearly seen on the top of a hill. Menhirs like this have been found all over Cheshire, Staffordshire and Derbyshire and seem to line up with round lumps of stone ('pudding' stones) in between, which seem to come at intermediate points between the large stones. There are also various crosses, but these latter are peculiar to this side of Derbyshire, this part of Cheshire and Staffordshire only. It is not certain exactly what these are, but they do seem to line up with the other stones. The Carne Stone seen from Buxton Road should prove very interesting if permission could be obtained to excavate it properly (it later was). If relics such as the Bridestones, Arbor Low and one or two other well known marks like Sandbach crosses are plotted on to a map, it is possible, she said, to link them in a straight line which beams on to Snowdon and it is quite possible that this was a very early prehistoric trackway from marker to marker. Very often the older standing stones have been replaced by a cross. The old straight tracks were the earliest prehistoric ways of travelling from place to place, she said.

She continued that prehistoric man did a great deal of trading and stone axes have been found in excavations very far from the places where the stone was quarried. Likewise there are flint implements of a variety which could not possibly have been made

And sheep may safely graze.The land to the front of this picture is where the 'Carne' stone once proudly stood - on a navel of the Earth Mother

Mrs May Carne, the larger than life character who experienced a violent thunderstorm as she was researching around the Carne Stone - as also did a local farmer when the stone was removed from its position where it had been for thousands of years.

near the place where they were found and so must have been traded from elsewhere. This, she ascertained, points to the possibility of there being a trade route linking these finds which, plotted on to a one inch Ordnance Survey map do form a straight line - a ridgeway.

May Carne went on that ridgeways frequently pass by tombs and barrows and it is difficult to establish which came first, the track or the tomb. She said there is a very good Ridgeway starting at the Carne Stone from where the stones make a trail straight up the map from south to north, passing a barrow on top of a hill at Further Harrop Fold Farm, Pott Shrigley. This barrow is in a field where there is a large stone square filled with trees and said to be a

The barrow in the field at Pott Shrigley

burial ground for Black Death victims and this ridgeway can be traced right up to the Scottish borders. Markers appear about every three miles and would be visible to the naked eye - 'pudding' stones may be found at intervals in between to show the right track. These roads, she said, often became salt ways later and one such track runs right to the barrow at Further Harrop by a stone 'cross' behind the Highwayman Inn at Rainow - lining up with the ridgeway - now only traces of a green road remain. Romans then built military roads on top of the older roadways, for example the Leek to Buxton road. She went on to say that Mercian crosses are very often found in pairs like the Bow Stones and, she says, were possibly markers between two different sets of land owners but it is not sure whether they were the original stones or replacements.

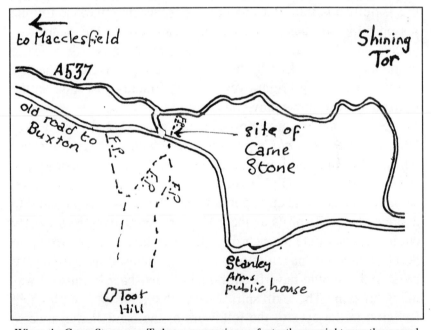

Where the Carne Stone was. Today, a concessionary footpath goes right over the mound it stood upon. Excavation has shown there to be a flat paved area under the boggy ground. It was obviously a site of great importance.

I would say here that we differ on a few points. Her conjecture of the 'old straight tracks' is correct in that they are straight lines between the points and could have been highways in part, but they are also lines of powerful earth energy. May Carne was not aware of this Earth Energy but I know that, had she been so, she would have carried out much invaluable research. I disagree that the Mercian crosses were possibly markers for land owners - but would agree wholeheartedly that they replaced ones that were there before. Where they remain in situ, at the Bow Stones, Cluelow Cross and at a little-known spot on Prestbury Road at Upton Priory, just outside Macclesfield, they are all on powerful energy lines. It is no coincidence. She does also say that they are quite likely to have been Monastic boundary markers and this is quite possible. But I feel they were used as markers for one reason only - because they were there already. In the same way, many burial mounds became markers because they were prominent landmarks and it is quite common for boundary drystone walls to go right over the top of them - just look on the horizon and see how many you can spot!

She certainly whetted my appetite with what she had to say later. I quote: *"Most old large stones were believed to contain very bad spirits"* and said it was quite possible that the cross or plague stone at Greenway, Higher Sutton, must have been a very 'bad' stone indeed and it is quite possible that the cross was put there to exorcise the evil spirits as there is a very attractive cross clearly cut in a round circle on each side. She is right and she is wrong. In point of fact the 'pagan' stone was Christianised by carving the cross and it would have been thought to be 'bad' because it was not Christian. The evil spirits were the remnants of the Old Religion in the eyes of the followers of the New. Perhaps we're agreeing on this after all!

An article in the Macclesfield Advertiser of June 1974 is

The little-known ancient 'cross' in a hedgerow at Upton Priory

worth quoting from the point of view that it refers to more of these old trackways, but it does tend to confuse these lines. Some are undoubtedly old thoroughfares but some never have been. They have 'markers' on them not to guide the traveller along but to penetrate the earth to use the energy that comes from within and, also, to revitalise that energy. Again, I am fully aware that some will not agree with me - fads and fancies come and go and they fade into the next craze - but the evidence is there. This energy can still be drawn upon and, more often than not, it is a good and kind energy - a powerful source of healing.

The article says a well-defined track on lower ground passes through the 'obelisk' at Knutsford, on the road to Chelford, passes close to a tumulus near Capesthorne Hall and through the ancient cross at Gawsworth. The writer is clearly seeing a straight line in this case and, therefore, thinking it is a highway. It isn't unless it could be looked upon as a highway of energy.

It then refers to ley lines and classes them the same as the old tracks, just as Alfred Watkins first did early in the twentieth century. It says that as highway robbery became more prevalent the ancients made use of ridgeways which did not keep to an absolute straight line but kept to the higher, safer, land. To a degree this is also correct, but those ridgeways are a lot older than given credit for. They are the original highways just as others that have followed the old straight tracks between places of religious and cultural and healing importance.

It tells of a well defined ridgeway that passes from the south in Staffordshire, near Ashbourne at Mapleton, to Ilam, Ford Wetley, High Cross at Bradnop, Stile House near Leek, Dieulacres Abbey just north of Leek, Axstone Spring, Heaton (where an old stone used to stand), Wincle Grange, Cleulow Cross, the Bullstone or Bullstrang at Hammerton Knowl, Greenway Cross, High Moor (again, where a stone used to be but has now 'fallen' into a field),

The stone behind the Highwayman at Rainow.

Ridgegate and an offset gate on Charity Lane, the Carne Stone, Blue Boar Farm, the stone at the back of the Highwayman, the Bowstones at Lyme Park, and on across Saddleworth as far as Halifax and then the borders.

But some of these stones are not on tracks of any description. They do, in all instances that I have noted, appear on energy lines, however (discovered in every instance with either divining rods or a pendulum). In any landscape there are some that are merely boundary markers - usually between parishes. A very good example is up by the

The pub sign!

The 'cross' at Cauldon Lowe.

Bullstrang where stones are carved with 'W' and 'S' for Wincle and Sutton. Many are not. At first glance they do not seem to perform any useful purpose whatsoever. One such is at Flash, close by the bridge over the River Dane. It stands alone in a field and does not appear to be marking a boundary or an ancient trackway but, again, it is penetrating the earth where an energy line runs. And at Cauldon Lowe - where there are many traditions of the fairy people having danced throughout the centuries - there is another stone 'cross'. The pub across the road is called, not surprisingly, 'The Cross' yet it has as its sign a Crusader with a cross on his breastplate. How sad - the cross the pub was named after stands proudly in a field just across the road!

Temple to the Sun God?

Harold Bode is a highly respected retired headmaster who has, throughout his life, been a keen walker and cyclist. Indeed, he has cycled the length and breadth of this island raising money for charity and publicising good causes. I remember he fought long and hard to save an ancient farmstead called 'The Dumkins' on the Staffordshire and Cheshire borders (a place where a local farmer once saw footprints believed to be those of a panther or similar creature). Some years ago he brought out a booklet giving details of what he thinks may very well be a Sun Temple on Ipstones Edge. And in 1980 a local paper, the Evening Sentinel, published an article about his find.

Harold wrote in the paper that while he and his wife were walking towards Ipstones Edge one day he noticed some stones *"in a woodland that primitive people might venerate"*. In the next field he saw large stones scattered about and he realised they were walking through what he thought was a "prehistoric temple". He and his wife returned to that spot on June 20th of that year and saw that from a stone he termed the "Sun" stone, the sun set over

Sharpcliffe Rocks and, after more visits, he drew a plan that vividly portrayed his theory.

This "Sun Stone" is described as a "rough quadrilateral" with its points facing the compass points, North, South, East and West. There is a hollowed out section in the south east position and this, when water fills it, reflects the mid winter sunrise. In addition, Harold noticed a groove running in a north westerly direction across the stone towards the direction of the midsummer sunset. On this direct line he also saw two marker stones, although woodland prevents them being sighted on Sharpcliffe Rocks.

To the east there is another stone and calculations and observations by Harold show it marks the equinox dawn sunrise. And that is not all by any means. He also came across a triangular pyramid-shaped stone to the south west and over this pyramid stone the full moon at midsummer would rise at its maximum. To the south there is yet another marker stone and also a cairn and these mark mid day and the full moon at midnight. There is another triangular stone to the west and this one indicates the Celtic festivals of Beltaine - now May Day - and Samhain - the time most now refer to as Hallowe'en. All this is quite remarkable but there is more. Harold has placed on record that west of north is yet another special stone and this one points to the cove within the woodland and it is hollowed out to hold water. At the equinox sunset the sun would be seen to set behind this cove and, in Harold's words, *"Strike fire out of the water."* There is, almost north, a "much pitted" stone marking the zodiac. Harold notes that the equinox sun stone has been damaged - deliberately, it would appear - and trees and a drystone wall block the gap between the stones of the cove. In addition, he points out that hawthorns and newish woodland block the sight along the Sun Stone's groove to Sharpcliffe. If owners of the land, or others, were aware of the significance of these stones over the past centuries then it is more than likely they would have been obscured

73

The Sun Temple at Ipstones,
discovered by Harold Bode

deliberately. That's the way it used to be.

It must be pointed out that the stones are in a meadow owned by Sexton Farm, Ipstones Edge and permission must be sought to inspect them. Further, the cove is situated within woodland owned by White Hough Farm, Ipstones. Do, please, honour the ownership of this land if you should wish to visit the site.

The very name "Ipstones" suggests the area has been named after certain stones that have, quite obviously, been looked upon as exceedingly special. The old spelling of the area was "Yp" Stones and to what this name referred we can now only guess. But Harold's theory regarding the Sun Temple certainly holds water - just like the hollowed out rocks there! - and it could very well be that this special site gave its name to the area. This would have been a place venerated by the Ancients - a place for pilgrimage. A place holy to the Old Ones and a place we should be aware of today.

Mysteries from the Earth

The Earth upon which we live holds many mysteries. I doubt if we will ever solve them all and, quite honestly, I hope we don't solve them all. We would then be as wise as the Old Ones who placed most of these mysteries underground and the Earth would be stripped of her mystery. Just like a beautiful woman it should be allowed to retain this cloak of secrecy - it's more exciting. Throughout the years men have dug into the ground to uncover "treasure" of one form or another. That Victorian gentleman, Mr Bateman, travelled up and down the Three Shires uncovering ancient burial mounds, for instance. Not that he dug them himself - he and his pals would sit and watch, no doubt accompanied by a glass or two of port and the odd pheasant paté - while the specially hired labourers went straight for the middle of these mounds, finding the calcified remains of a warrior chief or a Wise Man and the special possessions buried with them - and added them to the long list of "booty". Goodness only knows what else was destroyed along the way. But he wasn't alone in this, it became quite the thing to do in Victorian times and it is on record that "certain Victorian gentlemen" were responsible for excavating a tumulus on Macclesfield Common. It is now believed that the particular one they dug was at Tegsnose - or Teggs Nose as some, including the County Council and Ordnance Survey would have it called. This spelling is wrong, but who am I to argue?

Tegsnose is a special place or, rather, it was a special place. Over the years there has been much quarrying for the special stone within the earth and over recent years it has been "landscaped" to a degree to make a Country Park. This is no bad thing in a way for it enables many more to enjoy the countryside than ever before, although I have mixed feelings about "country parks". They are pasteurised versions of the real thing - how better to have left the land more in its natural rugged glory but still made it accessible (I must get off my soapbox!).

75

The country park - once the home of the Fairy People?

The name Tegsnose or Teggs Nose could possibly be derived from the shape of the hillside, resembling the nose of a sheep - a Teg in Old English. Or, it could be from the Old Celtic and here we have something much more interesting for Tylwyth Teg (terlooth teig) means the Fair Family - the place where a family of fairies live or lived.

How I recall so vividly one of those magical mornings that I'm sure we have all experienced, when the sun was shining on the dew and the air was crisp and clear. The skylark was singing as Hilary and I walked along one of the old quarry roads alongside the country park and the dew was twinkling in the heather, reflecting the sunshine. But this twinkling seemed to show something darting in and out of the heather - could it have been fairy folk? I'd like to think so but logic tells me no. It was most certainly the twinkling of sunlight but it showed how easily the superstitious could have mistaken it for the Fair People.

On the southern side of Tegsnose there still stands this tumulus excavated by those Victorian gentlemen. Today its looks like a miniature volcano because of the huge hole in its middle but its location is outstanding. To the south it commands a spectacular view of the Mow Cop hill, Sutton Common with the communications tower now astride it and the pyramid-shaped Shutlingslow (again, not 'Shutlingsloe' as the Ordnance people think). Round to the West is Bosley Cloud and then over to the Cheshire Plain and the Peckferton Hills and the commanding hill at Beeston; then turn more northwards and the Pennines are in sight. All around there are landmarks that would have been of immense importance. To have been buried in such a spectacular spot, that person must have been of considerable importance. Was he or she the ruler of all that could be surveyed from that burial place? I think it highly likely.

The tumulus at the country park. It now resembles a mini volcano. Whoever was buried there was a very highly respected person - the spot commands a unique panoramic view of The Three Shires. These mounds were known as Fairy Hills.

77

These burial mounds have, throughout the centuries, been referred to as Fairy Hills. The flint arrowheads often dug from them were "fairy spears". They were never disturbed at one time, for fear of disturbing those fairies. Within these fairy hills there has been much treasure. Some of it has been the treasure so many of us crave - gold, silver and semi precious stones. But other treasure is far more priceless - the earthen pots shaped by the hands of a master potter some 3000 or more years ago; the flints made into weapons or tools - so prized by Neolithic people; the fossils that would have been personal treasures of these people (at Gawsworth, one tumulus was found to contain a fossilised shell. It would have been the personal possession of the person buried there. Something obviously very, very special to them). And much more.

Heart of Stone

At Leek, a heart carved from stone was once uncovered. Where Spring Gardens now stands, overlooking the Westwood Recreation Ground, there used to be a burial mound. It stood, like all the others, for over 3000 years until it was deemed necessary to build houses there. The name given to it was Cock Low - Low denoting a burial mound and "Cock" deriving from the word denoting "king" or ruler - the big boss! The expression "Cock of the North" is from the same roots. When the workmen moved in to destroy Cock Low the first of many loads taken from it revealed its construction to be of layers of a strangely white sand alternating with black charcoaled sand.

In *Memorials of Old Staffordshire* mention is made of this and the writer said:

> Whether the mound had been used for sacrifices or had been simply the place where charcoal had been burnt seemed doubtful. But some interesting discoveries were made. Near the top of the mound on the South side a fine urn, with a double lip for carrying it, tumbled out one September day, falling to pieces, but displaying its contents. These were

first of all, strange to say, a little heart neatly carved in stone and then a small parcel of hacked or chopped up bones - both animal bones and bits of a child's skull. The story told by these things appeals to one's deep sympathies for some poor mother long ago bereaved of her child by cannibal workers at the mound.

This is fanciful in the extreme. Nearer to the mark would be the fact that it was a child buried in the mound and the animal bones were guardians - there to help the dead child on its way to the next life. But why a stone heart? It was often the tradition to bury someone's heart at another place that was their spiritual spot, somewhere they had received great enjoyment from being. And then a substitute heart was placed in the burial mound.

The book goes on to relate that lower down in the mound, pockets of charcoal were found and on the ground level was a mass of stones, not quite a circle, dyed red with the washing of rains through the red sand above them. For the mound had lacked that usual envelope of clay by which so many remains have been preserved elsewhere.

But a further yield was made. A drain was driven along the foot of the mound and in the sand which had filled it were many traces of a brilliant light blue, which Sir Thomas Wardle (one of the main mill magnates of the time in that town) examined and pronounced to be woad - the material used by early Britons for tattooing their faces and for covering their bodies. Blue has long been classed as a mystical colour and is used in healing to this day. It is not beyond the bounds of possibility that the woad was placed in the mound for this purpose - in some way an attempt to heal the body, or perhaps even bodies, that lay there within that mound - a mound with a stone circle, or probably an oval-shaped circle in it at one time. It must have been a very impressive sight and it is very sad indeed that it had to be destroyed without more work being carried out on it so that future generations could have gained more knowledge about what lay therein. Perhaps the circle had been covered over at some date. But it was the same throughout the three counties and throughout many more counties up and down the country. I am sad to say that it is still going on. The cement works at Cauldon Low have quarried out great hills that are now gone forever. These were the hills where ancient man not only buried his dead but where the fairy people were said to have their meetings. Whatever lay asleep under those places has now been destroyed - not with any ill intent but purely because the quarry workers did not realise what secrets those hills held. But perhaps the spirits remain. And the same can be said of many other quarries throughout Derbyshire, although at Wormhill - a name signifying the Earth Spirit, the Wyrm or Dragon if ever there was one - there has been extensive use made of the local stone in the area around and this has destroyed much, but the village itself, that is home to a memorial to canal builder James Brindley, is delightful. What a surprise that this place, home to the Earth Spirit or dragon, should have its quaint church dedicated to Saint Margaret - who is often depicted as defeating a dragon. This, surely, is extending coincidence to the extreme, and I truthfully feel that the village's name and its church's saint are there for one in the same reason. Thankfully, therefore, much HAS been saved. Perhaps not for the right reasons, but it has been saved, and for that we must be grateful.

Take, for instance, the enigmatic, strangely carved stones that are housed in the Iron Age exhibition at Buxton Museum. What is the secret these stones are hiding? When a vault at Mouselow was opened in 1840 these stones, with carvings upon them that have never been deciphered, were discovered. In recent times it has been found that when they are placed near to computers and other electrical apparatus the equipment goes haywire or will not work at all. Archaeologists and scientists are baffled.

And what secrets did the locally named Serpentine Stones hide? These stones are clearly marked on eighteenth and nineteenth century maps all around the Tegsnose area outside Macclesfield and on the way towards Buxton. Now they have been removed, in all probability because they were getting in the way of ploughs. On the Victorian maps they form serpent-like lines. And that is it. We know nothing more, except they were of sufficient importance to be marked on maps. What size they were and what shape they were we know not, but we do know where they were. I and Maurice Winnell have wandered high and low around the area, especially around Rulow (again a name denoting a burial site) but little or nothing is there now. Perhaps we may have discovered one stone by an underground reservoir off the Old Buxton Road but, then again, perhaps not. Even if we have, it is but one of many. I am aware that one of them was removed in the early 1990's when a gate entrance was enlarged.

I wish I had known about these so-called Serpent Stones (probably twenty in all) sooner than I did and then one of them, at least, could have been either preserved or recorded. Did the shape they made denote the Wyrm or Serpent - the Earth Powers? It can only be conjecture, for when they were removed they probably retained some power and this has gone with them. Another sadness.

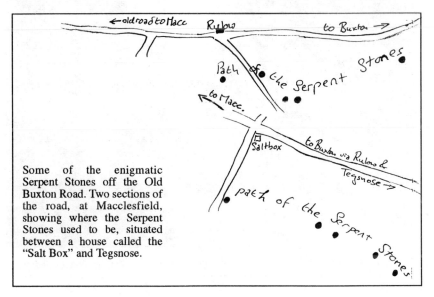

Some of the enigmatic Serpent Stones off the Old Buxton Road. Two sections of the road, at Macclesfield, showing where the Serpent Stones used to be, situated between a house called the "Salt Box" and Tegsnose.

Cauldon Low - once the home of the fairy people and the burial place of the Ancients. Today, quarrying has defeated it.

Wormhill, once the home of the Earth Spirit, and where the church is dedicated to a dragon slayer.

5
MYSTICAL MIDDLE OF THE THREE SHIRES

Of Three Shire Heads strange tales are told - so says a poem by the late Walter Smith about this amazing land. He is absolutely right. Many a strange tale has been told, and many will continue to be. This is the Land where the mountains and moorlands meet the meres and the murmuring rivers meandering to the seas - rivers that once possessed goddesses, if our forefathers are to be believed, and mountains whose rocks were the scenes of sacrifices and many a ritual that would seem strange indeed today. As I have mentioned, some of these rituals are still alive but they are kept 'below the surface', away from prying eyes. There is no longer any human or animal sacrifice made, but the sacred aspects of the rituals certainly do remain. I know, I have witnessed them. The fires are still lit and the flames still burn in the hearts of some.

One of the spots in the Mystical Middle is the area of Higher Sutton, around Meg Lane. This was once the fringe of the ancient Macclesfield Forest - a sparsely populated hunting ground for royalty - and now a new kind of forest has grown up thanks to the planting efforts of the original Macclesfield Corporation Water Works. It was within this forest that suicides were buried on the crossroads atop Standing Stone Hill. Remnants of this standing stone are still within a drystone wall - walk up to the path towards Shutlingslow and it can be found to the left - and it was among the hills in these parts that members of the Meg Lane gang of coiners dispersed themselves during the latter half of the eighteenth century. They were a class of violent criminals who carried out daring robberies to obtain gold and silver plate to be melted down for their private 'mint'. The headquarters for their nefarious business was in Meg Lane Farm, now known as Meg Lane End. It

The Coining Machines

is a delightful place today. From the gardens there are grand views of the s u r r o u n d i n g countryside.

It is stated that the gang was finally betrayed by a young girl who lived with one of the gang at a lonely farmhouse. On the information she laid down with the authorities the gang was broken up and it is recorded that several of them were hanged at Chester. It was at Meg Lane End that the powerful coining machines, worked by a screw, were kept for many a year. These punched out the impressions and the metal dies that were used for making the impressions. It used to be possible to make out the heads of George II and George III on some of the dies that were kept at Meg Lane while on another was the impression of Britannia used for the reverse side of the coins. The dies had the initials 'I.H.' and these are said to be those of one Isaac Heath who kept a smithy where the Ryles Arms pub is now situated in Hollins Lane, Sutton. His ghost remains there, it is said. The original machines and dies were found many years ago in a well at Meg Lane Farm and it is conjectured that when the gang learned that the law was closing in on them their leader threw them in the well.

The Ryle's Arms, formerly a smithy where the blacksmith was a member of the notorious gang. Is it his ghost that haunts the pub today?

There is a poem called *Spell bound*, a tale of Macclesfield Forest by a writer who used the pen name of "Redgirdle" and part of it is entitled *The Forest Fay*. It was published many years ago. It tells the story of the Meg Lane gang and the exploits of Black Hugh Raven a member of the gang who, when he spoke in anger, "his teeth gnashed and the fire from his eyeballs flashed". It tells of beacons being lit on Hollinsclough to warn of pending danger and gives the following description of Meg Lane:

South East of Hollins you may trace an old, a lone, and sullen place, hid in the gloomy woods that grow throughout the glen that lies below.
Who wills a nearer view to gain must thread a dark and narrow lane; entered by passing through a wood, and o'er the mill stream's murmuring flood.
At this lane end there stands alone the gloomy house all built of stone. Thick rugged walls of dark grey rock, skill, taste and time alike do mock. The narrow holes for windows made to let in light seen half afraid.

It was here that dark Hugh Raven dwelt with his sole

companions - two men, and two dogs called Rock and Chase *"the men as wild and fierce as Hugh."* The writer tells of a secret cavern in which were hid the hoards of cups, flagons, *"pieces of rich and costly plate, which nobles used in times of state"* and of the furnace in which the metal was melted down. The poem describes the throwing of the machines and dies into the well:

> Quick all the treasure down is cast; the coining engines, left 'til last, he grasped with giant strength to throw, and dashed them down the steps below.
> Thus having sunk th' ill-gotten hoard, he seized his cap, girt on his sword, unloosed the chains of Rock and Chase and swiftly hurried from the place.

Today it is not quite clear where the well is situated. Some say it was the one by the side of Meg Lane End House and others that it was across the yard. One thing is certain - Hugh must have been a very strong man to lift the machines himself. Eventually the Meg Lane coiners were captured and hanged at Chester. I have heard it said that a ghost haunts the house. It may or may not be one of the gang. There is also a ghost that haunts the Ryle's Arms. Perhaps this is the blacksmith who used to be part of the gang. Perhaps it is someone else. There are many homes within the Middle of the Three Shires that are haunted. Some of them we shall look at further within these pages.

Had this gang of coiners anything to do with the notorious Flashmen who counterfeited coins in much the same way? Flash stands right next to Three Shires Head and, as you are aware, the Flash Coiners escaped capture by hopping from Shire to Shire over the River Dane. This area of Sutton and the area of Three Shires are not far from each other. In fact, if you were a native of the area and you were used to trudging those hills then it would be a matter of a mere few minutes hike from one to the other. Either it was a great coincidence that two such gangs existed side by side

d he laughed - he said there was nothing there. H
e he was and they saw the horse get nearer ar
Then he jumped into the ditch by a drystone wall
e horse just as it was upon him. They all rushed
y he was pretty shaken up and somewhat bruise
noticed what happened to horse and rider, "they ju
said mother.

valks the ruins of his folly

ained apparitions abound in the Mystical Middle o
res, and here we simply must look at Old Abraham
built (and rebuilt and rebuilt) Folly Mill. Its ruins, a
Langley's Mr Cyril Dawson, stand in a hauntingly
ley covered with aged oaks and other mature trees
ht penetrates the leaves during summertime and it i
hat some travellers feel ill at ease when they walk by
ver the years a number of people have seen a man hard
uilding these ruins. They all report they have seen a
of figure - a very old man with a white stubbly beard
g leather trousers and a greyish vest. Is this Abraham
e folly the mill was?
are numerous follies up and down the country - the
p Mow Cop is a fine example - and most arc houses,
numents and the like situated in out-of-the-way
le or foolish positions; or there is something grotesque
ldings themselves.
e is a farm in Bosley, on the Mins, that used to be called
olly but now is Upton Fold Farm and as the farm is situated
and remote position, with - at one time - bad access it may
for granted that it was called a folly on that account.
gdale is the road that runs from Cleulow (or Clulow)
Allgreave Bridge. On the Cross side of the bridge, a road

or they are one and the same. Certainly, I have seen a photograph of the machine found at Meg Lane used to describe the Flash Coiners' instruments. Just one more mystery, I think, to add to the list.

Why have there been so many sightings of ghosts or wandering spirits in the area around Sutton and over to the Three Shires? Many of these have been of men on horseback - not the usual highwaymen so beloved of the romantic storytellers but wild looking men in an unkempt state galloping along, often with a storm lamp in their hand. Are they running from something or someone?

David Hemingway is a computer operator, a person with a logical mind and someone who is not prone to 'seeing things'. He does not drink to any excess, a couple of pints of real ale a week are about his limit. On the night of Thursday, January the fifth, 1995, he was in his car passing by Cleulow Cross, that man-made mound with a stone monolith perched atop it. He was driving back from Wildboarclough and took the road towards Sutton. Just as he approached the brow of a hill, (and here he admits he was speeding somewhat, but there was nothing else on the road - or so he thought) he saw the head of a man approaching over the brow. Then he saw it was a man on horseback, galloping up the centre of the road at great speed. The man had a long black beard and he wore a three-cornered hat. Horse and rider rode straight towards him. He braked, skidded and stopped with a screech of brakes and his reflexes made him place his head down, his chin touching his chest.

"I thought the horse was a goner for sure", David told me later. "It and the rider were still coming at me and I thought they couldn't stop." He raised his head and the animal's chest was towering above him, still riding forwards.

"That's it, I thought, it's going to hit the bonnet," he said. "I put my hands to my head and dropped down as far down to the floor as I could. I was between the seat and the pedals, kneeling on the floor expecting an almighty crash."

Nothing happened. He looked up and there was nothing. No-one was about on the road. Then, he noticed a car's headlights illuminated the sky and he heard the noise of an engine. A car was on its way from Sutton and as it approached it stopped. David realised he was in the middle of the road and the driver could not get by. Its headlights flashed and the horn peeped. David sat up and drove to the side of the road. The car peeped at him in anger and drove on and David got out. He left the headlights on and looked around but could see nothing. And that was it. No sign of a horse or a rider.

I recall exactly the same thing being witnessed by the late Jimmy Panayi who was the landlord of the Rose and Crown at Allgreave at the time. He had a mini-bus and used to drive it into Macclesfield to collect customers for his restaurant so they could have a drink without worrying about driving. I was a regular customer at his restaurant in those days and recall him returning with his minibus one night looking very shaken indeed. He thought the had killed a horse and its rider in exactly the same spot that David had witnessed the phantom horseman. Jimmy had come head to head with horse and rider and had stopped his vehicle but the animal and its rider kept galloping towards him. Jimmy put his hands over his eyes. When he took them away, nothing was there.

And many have seen strange sights around Three Shires Head. A Japanese tourist came face to face with a horse and rider one summer's day in 1992. The tourist and his wife and three children drove their hired car to Flash and had a meal at the New Inn. They asked about local walks and were directed to the Three Shires Head and off they went. They returned some hours later and

the landlady heard agita
out of the window and
after ten minutes or so th
the family were in the ca
her dog and walked towa
walked by. She noticed th
had her hand on his brow.
if everything was all rig
knowledge of English - said
the landlady invited them al
and asked if they would lik
she asked what was wrong.
walking down a path towards
racing up towards them. The
and all the family moved to
seem to notice the oncoming

From the top of Standing Stone in idyllic days at th
planted. Picture courtesy of Harry Hancox, form
Langley.

him to move an
remained when
nearer to him.
he had seen th
father and saw
None of them
disappeared"

Old Abraham
Those unexp
the Three Sh
the man who
depicted by
beautiful va
Little sunlig
no wonder
this spot. O
at work re
similar sor
and wearin
Day, whos
There
'castle' ato
mills, m
inaccessib
in the bui
The
Young's
in a high
be taken
Lo
Cross t

turns off Longdale in the direction of Wincle. Up this road, in a very short distance, Longdale Farm is passed, then almost immediately there is a turning to the left to Allmeadows Farm, only a few yards away. Pass through the farmyard, cross a stile, and go down a cart track which soon becomes a smooth grassy track, bear left and keep by a wall (avoiding a turn to the right which leads to Bartomley Farm, Hogs Clough and Wincle) and then through a wall and make straight for Folly Mill - an old paper mill in ruins - by a sinuous downpath, supreme in beauty, overlooking the gorge of a stream.

The late Mr Walter Smith described what comes next as follows: *"When once the path is gained the visitor is simply astonished at the beauty, and presently, at the uniqueness of the scene."*

He continued that deep down in the wooded gorge at the foot of a cliff called Gibbons Cliff are the ruins of the old mill on the verge of the Tor Brook. The gorge is deeply shaded by the trees of Gibbons Cliff Wood on the mill side of the stream, and of Allgreave Wood on the opposite bank, while a little lower down stream, the gorge abruptly terminating, comes the confluence of the Tor Brook and the Dane.

The old mill, having been partially thrown down, was then left neglected and where men once toiled it is now hardly possible to pick one's way on account of the usual growth about waterside ruins - coltsfoot, the nettle, the butterbur of prodigious size, and wild shrubs of various kinds. The last descent to the mill is by a number of slippery steps and great care should be taken in moving about the tottering ruin.

A mural tablet to the memory of Abraham Day in Wincle Church points unmistakably to the Elder of Folly Mill, says Walter. On the tablet it is stated that Abraham died in 1835 at the age of 95 years. From this we may deduce that if he built the mill in middle life it would be about 1790 when he was 50 years of age.

Abraham Day married a member of the Allgreave family of Mason and seems to have died childless, but there is a tradition in the Day family (descendants of Abraham's brother) that the mill was the third to be built there. According to the tradition the first mill Abraham built was washed away by a flood, and also the second.

He declared his intention to build a third but his wife said it would be folly to do so and that if he did she would go to bed, and stay there she did until she died in 1826 aged 76. Whether this behaviour was due to mere perversity or on account of depression and illness we are not told. It is evident that Abraham was an extraordinary man of strong physique, indomitable will and tenacity of purpose.

Not much seems to be known about the subsequent history of the mill. Presumably, Day worked it himself as a paper mill but at one time it was worked by Thomas Hope of White Lee, Wincle, whose name appears in an 1825 directory as a paper maker. Day's name occurs in the same directory: "Abraham Day, Allmeadows, farmer and land owner."

In 1849 the mill was to be let and was described as the

Folly Grove Paper Mill, Wincle, near Macclesfield, with Water Power and machinery for Manufacturing and Finishing Paper. Apply to Mr Matthew Longden (wheelwright) on the premises of Mr Thomas Slack (farmer) Sutton, near Macclesfield.

The mill used to manufacture coarse paper, brown or blue, as used by grocers or ironmongers. Because it was built *'down a hole almost inaccessible'*, to and from which horses and carts had to drag the raw materials and the finished article - an almost impossible task - surely this was why it was named as a folly.

The mill has always been known as a Folly Mill but in 1849 we see an attempt to eliminate the unfavourable implication in the name by calling it *Folly Grove Mill* as though indicative of a mill in a leafy grove, and with no suggestion of foolishness about the mill itself. The mural tablet in Wincle Church records the death of Abraham Day's wife and also Abraham himself, and the following verse appears under Abraham's name:

> *Our life hangs by a single thread*
> *Which is cut off when we are dead,*
> *Time was I stood as thou does now*
> *And viewed the dead as thou does me.*
> *But time will come when thou shalt be*
> *And others stand and look on thee.*

Such is the nature of that valley that there have been sightings of other mysterious things as well. I have been told of a large cat-like

Folly Mill at Allgreave - with thanks to Cyril Dawson

93

animal in the area - a footprint was found at the nearby ruins of The Dumkins - and this is where some say they have seen the Fair People - the fairies. Travel over to Swythamley and there are traditions of fairies and also of witches.

Over on the Derbyshire side at Axe Edge and beyond a tradition still remains of a wandering soul who cannot find its resting place. And thereby hangs a tale....

Wanderer on the Moorlands

Throughout the wild moorlands between Macclesfield and Buxton, Buxton and Leek and Leek and Ashbourne, there is a tradition. It is of the "Wandering Jew" and it is a tale that was told in many a lonely farmstead. I have heard it told by four different families around the Axe Edge area; I have had it related to me by a farmer from Wildboarclough and it is documented by John Aubrey (1626-97) in his work *Miscellanies* as being told at Ipstones. His work says:

> Anno 165- At ----- in the *Moorlands in Staffordshire,* lived a poor old Man, who had been a long time Lame. One *Sunday* in the Afternoon he being alone, one knocked at his Door: he bade him open it and come in. The Stranger desired a Cup of Beer; the Lame Man desired him to take a Dish and draw some, for he was not able to do it himself. The Stranger asked the poor Old Man how long he had been ill? The poor Man told him. Said the Stranger I can cure you. Take two or three Balm Leaves steeped in your Beer for a Fortnight, or three Weeks, and you will be restored to your Health; but constantly and zealously serve God. The poor Man did so, and became perfectly well. This Stranger was in a Purple-shag Gown, such as was not seen or known in those Parts. And no Body in the Street (after Even Song) did see any one in such a colour'd Habit. Dr Gilbert Sheldon (since Arch-Bishop of Canterbury) was then in the Moorlands and justified the Truth of this, to Elias Ashmole Esq; from whom I had this Account.....

Jennifer Westwood in *Albion - A Guide to Legendary Britain,* Granada Publishing, 1985, says that the earliest recorded mention of this mysterious figure comes from Matthew Paris (1200-59).

Axe Edge - still bleak and beautiful - home to the legends of The Wanderer.

This figure was reported all over Europe in the Middle Ages and then there came a period when a number of people were actually wandering around bleak and isolated areas posing as "Wandering Jews", presumably for monetary gain.

This figure personifies the image of the outcast of God and features in a considerable amount of folklore in different disguises - like The Wild Hunt and, indeed, the Flying Dutchman. The Wild Hunt is brought nearer to home by the traditions of the Hounds of Hell who came in search of the body of the Abbott of Dieulacres Abbey near to Leek.

In search of Hobgoblins

The Brothers Grimm wrote 'The Elves' as one of their many fairy tales. This work was translated into English about the year 1823 or a little later and it bears an uncanny resemblance to a Derbyshire tale concerning a Hob.

Before looking into greater detail about Hobs, Hobgoblins and their other selves - Robin Goodfellow and Puck, for instance - here is the tale as related by S O Addy in 1895 in *Household Tales*.

Once upon a time there was a poor shoemaker who could not earn enough to keep himself and his family. This grieved him very much, but one morning when he came downstairs he found a piece of leather which he had cut out already made into a pair of shoes, which were beautifully finished. He sold those shoes the same day, and with the money he bought as much leather as would make two pairs of shoes. The next morning he found that this leather too had been made into shoes, but he did not know who had done it. In this way his stock of shoes kept always getting bigger. He very much wished to know who had made the shoes, so he told his wife he would stay up all night and watch, and then he found Hob Thrust at work upon the leather. As soon as Hob Thrust had finished a pair of shoes the shoemaker took them and put them into a cupboard. Immediately after that Hob Thrust finished another pair, which the shoemaker also took up and put away. Then he made first one pair of shoes and then another so fast that the little shop was soon filled with them, and as there was no more room in the house the shoemaker threw the shoes out of the window as fast as Hob Thrust could make them.

This Hob Thrust, or Hob Thrush or Hob Thurst, is a familiar figure all over Derbyshire and it also creeps into folklore just across the borders into Staffordshire and Cheshire. But it is mainly a Derbyshire figure. Often houses have the name Hob House or something similar and these were, originally, where Hob reigned. He was a mischief maker, a Puckish spirit, and sometimes he became known as Robin Goodfellow. The spirit of this Good Fellow also lives on in the traditions of Robin Hood - an Earth Spirit who was claimed by many localities - not least Nottingham.

But Robin or Hobbin is very much alive in the Three Shires. How dare Nottingham people claim him as their own! There is a

Hob Hurst House on the south west edge of Brampton East Moor. There is a track from Chatsworth to Upper Loads leading to it but there is, unfortunately, no public right of way. There is the name Hob Hurst given to a tumulus nearby.

And at the tiny but lovely village of Elkstone, close by Warslow, there is an area known as Hob Hay. In this place is Hob Hay Cottage, formerly the Post Office. This is an area. undoubtedly, that was home to this legendary Sprite or Spirit - if a legend it is. Over towards the Roaches, on what is now Ministry of Defence land, where the soldiers camp out on the bleak rocks and hide in the mist, there was Hob Farm. It is now one of the many derelict buildings in that area. Tradition has it that this was the scene of many a haunting - perhaps Hob or Puck up to his old tricks!

Let us quickly jump across the three shires to the Earlsway, the road taken by the Earls of Chester to their spiritual home at

Hob Hay Cottage at Elkstone in the Staffordshire Moorlands

Dieulacres Abbey, north of Leek. On this road, at a parting of the ways, there is a pub called the Coach and Horses. On the green in front of this hostelry is an ancient stone. This stone has many properties - it is aligned from the Bridestones to Beeston and it also served as an ancient marker stone. They have also been called 'pudding' stones in the past - stones marking the line in between standing stones. Many are now gone, unfortunately.

This particular stone has many traditions surrounding it - not least that it has been a meeting place for the fairy people. In addition, *The Gentleman's Magazine* 1801 says the stone was called Hob's Stone. You may recall my mentioning a character who used to live in the area known as 'Cap'. He was a fountain of

The magic stone on the Earlsway

98

knowledge concerning the local area's traditions and he, too, said this is where the Fair People would meet. He did not refer to it as Hob's Stone - he called it the Fairy Stone. Today, children play on the stone as their parents enjoy a pint or something else at the pub. It is fitting that they should do, for whether it is Hob or the Fairies who own that stone they both enjoy the company of children and, just like Peter Pan - a Hobgoblin if ever there was one - they don't want to grow up. Do any of us?

Just before we leave the goblins and fairies to look after themselves once more, let us take a look at a hill in the area that also has traditions of the fairy people and, also, a fairy tradition in a nearby town. As the motorist speeds along from Macclesfield to Leek, many take a short cut 'over the top' on the old Leek road. As they hurtle down towards the main road once again, there is a hill to the right. This is rather a special hill. It stands proud of the landscape and many are of the opinion that it is man-made. To the north of the hill is a wood, Barnswood, where scouts enjoy the freedom of the open air at their special camp. This hill is circular and, whenever a frost or snow lies on the ground, the hill divorces itself from the rest of the landscape. Often it is bedecked with snow or frost and the surrounding land is not. More importantly, it has large stones all around it and I cannot but wonder if they formed a stone circle, a circle of stones, at one time, around this hillock. Again, there are a number of local traditions connecting it with the 'little people' and it is by a stretch of road that is notorious for accidents. Whether or not this 'blackspot' is connected I shall leave you to decide.

In the magazine *Folklore*, volume 53/6 of 1942, W P Witcutt of St Mary's in Leek, wrote an article. In it, he mentioned that fairies were very often comnected with Neolithic and Bronze Age burial places or lowes. Thus the fairies danced on Cauldon Lowe, as in an oft-quoted poem, and on Christmas Eve those of Long

Low behind Castern Hall held high revel. The names of the lows, or lowes, also betray the connection. Thus Hob Hurst's House in Derbyshire (as we have already seen) and the now levelled Goodfellow Bank in Leek. The Good Fellows, again as we have seen, are the same as Puck or Hob and, again, connect with Robin. Mr Witcutt also wrote that they were associated with caves. One lived in Thor's Cave and a whole clan were to be found beneath Lud Church.

Could this hill we have just looked at be, in fact, an ancient burial place? If it is then it is certainly a very large one. No, I think it is not, but perhaps it is one of those man-made places built to fit in with the landscape - the swollen belly of the Earth Mother or, perhaps, the navel. Then again, like Mam Tor, it could be one of the mammary glands of the female goddess.

One of the large stones around the edge of the mysterious hill

The mysterious hill just outside Leek. It is, in all probability, a man-made structure and large stones have surrounded it, suggesting the possibility of a stone circle at the spot. There is a powerful earth energy line running through, and it has been said that the 'little people' used to live there. No-one knows for sure what its secrets are. Perhaps one day they will be uncovered, who knows?

Another of the enigmatic stones

At Rushton Church, built atop a swollen belly of the Earth Mother, an ancient stone still stands - but another was rolled away and has now disappeared. The Church is on a hill of the 'Good People' or 'Fellows' in local lore.

Part of the Old Way, around Bearda Hill at Swythamley. This is the route taken by the ragged army of the Young Pretender - the route of the Phantom Black Dogs - as we shall see.

6
PHANTOMS OF THE PRETENDER

The road South from Manchester through Macclesfield, Leek, Ashbourne and Derby and thence to London is a relatively modern one constructed, in the main, during the latter part of the eighteenth century when Turnpike fever was at its height. It took the speeding passenger and mail coaches from and to the towns along the route and it was used by the great family of hauliers from Adlington, Macclesfield and the moors around Buxton - the Pickfords - to transport their cargoes. But before then the route from North to South was a different one. For instance, from Macclesfield it went via Sutton and Wincle, by the Ship Inn, around Bearda Hill at Swythamley, over Gun and down to Leek via the grounds of the monastery. From there it went to Haregate Hall ('gate' denoting a routeway) via Bradnop - going by the ancient Egg Well - and through Waterfall by the cross and onwards to Ashbourne. Parts of the Old Way were utilised in the New - but not many.

This is the route taken by Prince Charles Edward Stuart, Bonnie Prince Charlie, the Young Pretender, as he headed his army of Highlanders and Lowlanders - the Barelegs, with kilts swirling, pipes playing and drums pounding - before that collection of old greybeards and youngsters not yet shaving, turned back at Derby. They were following a prophecy and they were following their spiritual leader spurred on by Right over Might. Had they continued southwards it is probable that the course of British history would have changed forever, but the retreat proved costly. They nearly all lost their lives in a massacre and their ghosts still haunt the Old Way, not wishing to surrender.

Not only do their ghosts haunt their melancholy meanderings

An illustration taken from Miller's Olde Leeke, 1891, entitled '*Over the Moors wi'*
Charley'. It shows some of the ragged army, the Barelegs. The advance and the retreat
across the moorland and Cheshire left behind Spectres, some say.

but the ghosts of Black Dogs are still sighted all along the route.
The Pretender's Phantoms are still with us. They haunt the paths
trodden by the Barelegs and they guard their graves. The Black
Dog phenomena has haunted the area between Macclesfield,
through Leek and on to Ashbourne for many a day. It raises its
head throughout the Three Shires (I have reported on the infamous
Black Dog of Bartomley, for instance, in a previous book and have
in my possession a photograph of such a beast there) but,
incredibly, the Spectre of the Black Dog can be traced all along the
path taken by the Pretender.

What is a phantom Black Dog? First of all, some would say
that these phantom animals only occur on ley lines. If they do,
then this may confirm a theory about the Old Straight Tracks,
wherein Old Ways follow earth energy lines. Certainly in this case,

anyway, for this Old Way is one trodden by thousands and thousands of feet over thousands of years. It is quite probable that, before humans came on the scene, it was a route used by the animals to and from their feeding and mating grounds. It is not a straight track in the accepted way, it twists and it turns but it twists and turns around high hills and holy places so that feet do not trample these spots. The apparitions of Black Dogs often occur near burial grounds and the sighting of the animal means impending death for someone of importance around that site. It may be the Vicar if the burial ground is by a church, or it may be the Lord of the Manor if the burial ground is on his land. It is not the person who sights the Phantom who is at risk of passing on to the next life but the person for whom the Phantom comes. A black dog used to be buried in the corner of a newly consecrated burial ground so that its spirit would wander, and not the spirit of the others buried there.

Sometimes Black Dogs appear at a place where a murder has been committed. Sometimes they appear where a suicide victim has been buried at a crossroads - the body placed there so that its soul cannot find the true path. One such place of suicides was at Standing Stone in Macclesfield Forest. Another, at Alderley Edge close by Windmill Wood is a spot that still registers black energy. It is a place where few animals will linger and, indeed, it is a place where most humans, certainly those who are only even remotely sensitive to 'atmospheres' will feel uncomfortable. I have dowsed this spot and could not wait to get away from it. The atmosphere closes in like a blanket; it is not a place for the faint hearted. There are other such places. One is Gun Hill - where public hangings took place - and one is at Ashbourne where the B5032 joined the A515 and A52. There is another behind the Cloud at Bosley, where the Earlsway is intersected by a road to Biddulph and such a crossroads of death used to be where the Green Man is now at

One of the Black Crossroads - this is close by Windmill Wood at Alderley Edge. It is now a place where there has been much mining for copper and today is little more than a couple of footpaths crossing but the atmosphere soon tells most people that it is not a place to linger.

Bottomhouse. Thankfully our reaction to suicide has now changed but the black blanket still cloaks the areas where these poor unfortunates were laid down. And some accused of witchcraft also found themselves buried at these crossroads so their souls would be forced to forever wander. Public gallows were, similarly, at the crossings of the ways.

One researcher into Black Dog legends - Ivan Bunn, who traced many in the East Anglia area - noticed that nearly all the apparitions occurred near to water, either the sea or rivers or on low-lying damp ground. Another researcher, this time around the Bournemouth region, noticed that over ninety per cent of Black Dog sightings and also sightings of UFOs were on ley lines.

But what about our own area? Let us move southwards from Adlington, just outside Macclesfield, along the route taken by the Pretender. Here there is the ancient Adlington Hall, a lovely black and white building for so long the home of the Legh family. In the

Civil War it was the site of a siege and it has its legends of hauntings. But James MacPherson, a 17 year old follower of the Pretender, is said to be buried in a field across from the entrance to the Hall. According to John Sleigh, a Leek historian, he was killed when a horse bolted and ran over him. There are two recorded instances of Black Dogs being sighted at the entrance to the Hall - one in 1799 when according to John Earles, a Macclesfield historian, a local farmer saw the dog and thought it warned of the death of Squire Legh. He does not seem to have come to any harm just around then, however. A further sighting was made early in the twentieth century by a Macclesfield schoolmaster, John Hyde. He was out walking, having alighted from the train at Adlington station, and as he strolled to the Hall he saw a Black Dog. He wrote in his diary - now in the possession of his family who live at Gorton in Manchester - that he had heard the tale of the Phantom Dog and hoped this would not bring ill fortune to the Leghs.

Some of the Scottish troops came South via Alderley, passing the stately home of the Stanleys. There is a tradition in the Stanley family that a black dog - a greyhound - foreshadowed death. This tradition was kept up in the name of one of the public houses on the Stanley Estate - the Black Greyhound. That pub has been shut a long time but across the road there is a Smithy known as the Black Greyhound Smithy (all the ale houses on the Stanley Estate were closed after Lord Stanley was being driven along the road by the Miners' Arms, now the Wizard, one evening and some miners who had been to the hostelry started to jeer at him).

The Pretender's Troops joined up again at Macclesfield and spent the evening of December 1st 1745 in that fine township and also the following day, leaving on December 3rd to march to Leek. Most of the people of the town were in church on that Sunday morning, presumably praying for their salvation, when they heard

The spot across the road from the entrance to Adlington Hall, where it has been recorded on at least two occasions that a Phantom Black Dog has been sighted. On both these occasions the Lord of the Manor does not seem to have come to any harm.

the sound of the approaching army which had come in two parts, one via Stockport and the other via Alderley Edge. Many of the townsfolk hastily left town, clutching their valuables. The army arrived at mid day and the quartermasters asked where Sir Peter Davenport's house was. Sir Peter was a relation of the Bromley Davenports of Capesthorne Hall and, it must be presumed, he was a supporter of the Pretender. He had a town house in King Edward Street, then Back Lane, and Sir Peter was not in. Whether he had fled or not we do not know, but his door was marked with the word 'Prince'. As a result his house was later vacated and used as the Grammar School. The Davenports of Capesthorne Hall - and of Bramall Hall - have been the subject of the Black Dog legend, especially at nearby Siddington Church.

They marched via Sutton - where the Black Dog has been seen as recently as March 1962, at a pool by Sutton Hall, and through to Wincle. Whether there is any tradition of a Scot being killed or buried near here I have not been able to ascertain.

108

Wincle is a village that has much tradition relating to the Pretender's troops stopping over at the Ship Inn and leaving behind some of their weapons there, including slingshot, two swords and an axe head. This is also a village that has a spectre of a headless woman and its church, built on a pre-Christian burial mound, has also been the venue for a Black Dog sighting or two. The late Mr Walter Smith, whom I have quoted in many of my books (I am a great admirer of his visions - he was way ahead of his time) referred to the Black Dogs in an article in the Macclesfield Times in 1933. He said they had been seen on several occasions and the local tradition has it that they always meant the impending death of the incumbent of the Parish. Sir Philip Brocklehurst, who owned nearby Swythamley Hall, once wrote to James Bateman of Knypersley Hall (and later of Biddulph Grange) and alluded to the same tradition. In a letter now in the possession of a lady at Wincle he said , *"I do not fear for the Parson even though the Black Dog has been witnessed at the Churchyard. I put it down to superstition and nothing more"*.

Close by to Swythamley and Wincle is the magical mystical and mysterious Lud Church, the cavernous cleft in the earth given its name from a Celtic deity. Here, the Prince is said to have slept the night in hiding. Whether during his advance or retreat it is not said, but if it is the truth then I would suggest it was during his retreat (he was said to have stayed at Royal Cottage on the Roaches but it is more likely some of his soldiers did. He would have been too conspicuous).

W P Witcutt, whose address was given as St Mary's, Leek, wrote on the *Folklore Magazine* volume 53 of 1946 that the "padfoot" or phantom black dog is common enough in the County of Staffordshire and his chief attribute seems to be the guardianship of graves. He also said that the retreat of Prince Charlie's army through the Moorlands in 1745 left quite a crop of these spectres. At Swinscoe, on the Leek to Ashbourne road, three Jacobites were ambushed and a phantom black dog guards their graves.

At the Oxhay Farm at Bradnop nearer Leek (at that time the Red Lion) two more Jacobites quarrelled in their cups and one slew the other. He is buried behind the farm and a black dog accordingly haunts the road. The writer continues:

> Another phantom of the same species was seen at the lane end near the much haunted Hermitage Farm in Ipstones parish in 1916. The Padfoot is also obscurely connected with wells, such as Indefont Well at Ipstones.

Where the Black Dog haunts at Bradnop.

So the memories of these Black Dogs still linger. And the fact that Bradnop has more than its share of them is of no surprise. This area around the village is one that contains much Earth Magic and Mystery. I have drawn attention to the Egg Well there on a number of occasions and would recommend a visit - but I would definitely not recommend partaking of its waters now. They were certainly healing waters at one time, but do not attempt to drink of them today - for your health's sake.

What is apparent about the area is evidence of what remains of the Old Religion. We have already looked at Hob, the Puckish Spirit of the Earth. He is alive and well around here at Hob Meadows

110

Wincle Church, built on a Neolithic Low and the scene of sightings of the phantom Black Dog.

below the Ridgeway known as Morridge - Moor Edge. Below Hob Meadows is a stone, known as the plague stone. There is a stone cross in a field below Morridge, also. This has been said to be a parish boundary marker and perhaps it may well be one today but I doubt if it has always been such a marker. This stone shaft stands guard over an area by the name of Wormlow, and Wormlow Farm centres upon it. Low, of course, denotes an ancient burial mound or a hill. Worm in this context denotes the supposed Serpent or Wyrm - the force of nature that the Church looked upon as Pagan and therefore evil. Both St George and St Michael have defeated this Worm in days long gone and behind the Egg Well there is Lady Meadows - an area devoted to the Lady - the Earth Mother, Briget, the goddess later to become Mary, the Sacred Lady.

111

The enigmatic stone shaft or cross in the middle of nowhere. It stands by the area known as Worm Low - a guardian over the Earth Spirit. Some say it once denoted a meeting place, but today there are no roads or paths leading to it

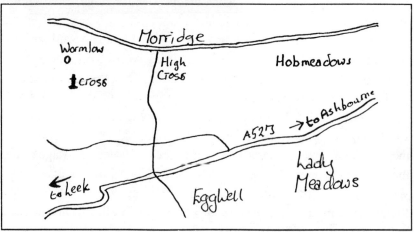

A map of the area around mystical Bradnop.

Rushton Spencer Well, now restored to former glory.

7
DARK FORCES AT A CELTIC WELL

Water fascinates me. As a child it was not surprising - water and small boys always attract each other - but later on I became drawn to wells, springs and rivers for reasons other than getting soaking wet and splashing about - I was lured by the spell of healing and the historical and religious associations water has. It soon became very clear that I and my schoolchums were not the only ones to have been fascinated by water. Many other people have been and many still are. Today we take water for granted, it is on tap, and while we may not agree with the prices we are charged for a commodity that is a gift from heaven, we are all guilty of accepting the life-giving revitalising force without much thought.

Not so thousands of years ago. Then it was indeed looked upon as a gift from heaven - a gift of the gods. And within it lurked the gods themselves who provided life and the means of living - healing - from within. There are many wells and springs still with us that are testament to the past. I have referred to several of the local ones before (not least the well at Rushton Spencer between Macclesfield and Leek - both a healing and a divination well - and I am most pleased to say that it has now been rescued and has been resuscitated and is now not only flowing again but a well dressing ceremony has been revived at it) and, indeed, I have also referred to the connections with that enigmatic and mystical tribe of Celts who inhabited this land. These connections are many and the clues are still all around. Take, for instance, a little known well or spring in the heart of the Southern Peak District that many motorists, walkers and cyclists will have travelled passed without giving it a glance. But it is a memory of the past that we should cherish - it denotes the Celtic preoccupation with life-giving waters and holds clues to the Cult of the Head and to worshipping the Earth Mother.

Take the car, the bus or the bike to Hartington first, before visiting the historical and holy watering hole to which I shall refer, and enjoy the village for what it is. Hartington today is a tourist trap, and quite rightly so. It has several tea rooms and several pubs that can supply sustenance to the visitor and there are the usual souvenir and craft shops, plus an elegance of quaint scenery - not to mention that delicious, nutritious and absolutely delightful Hartington Stilton cheese. It tastes like no other - a creamy blend with a thick crust. Those who have sampled it readily know why I am so in love with it and those who have not should try it. They don't know what they are missing.

Anyway, once the delights of Hartington have been sampled, travel along the road northwestwards towards tiny Pilsbury with the Long Dale on our right. There are several gates that have to be opened and closed, so a passenger willing to hop in and out of the car is a luxury I would recommend. About two miles along this track, by one of these gates, you will come across this Celtic relic - Luds Well, today shown as Ludwell.

Here is where memories of long ago still live - and where Hilary and I experienced dark forces, unconnected with the sweet waters that flow here, but very much in evidence. More of this later, but for now let us look at the shrine to the Celtic deity, Lud. This is the same god who gave his name to Lud Church on the Staffordshire/Cheshire border - the setting for the Arthurian poem Sir Gawain and the Green Knight. It is Lud who is manifested in Herne the Hunter and Cenunos the horned god - the life-giving force embroiled in the Green Man figures found at many of our churches, life over death portrayed along the way at Castleton when the Green Man rides at the Garland Day ceremony. Lud, who is still celebrated by some at Lughnasa, was a Nature God. To many he still is. He is also referred to as one of the Shining Ones

115

- who often lived on golden hills (Shining Tor at the Goyt Valley is a good example) and above the well there is a tumulus, a burial mound, known as Carder Low. Just by it is another sacred burial spot, a cairn. There is little or no doubt that for the area to be chosen to bury someone special then it must have been a valued place. Just anywhere would not do, it had to be somewhere the Earth Mother was in evidence and where powerful energy lines traverse the spot.

It had to be here. Three miles to the West there is a spot known as Ludburn, again a memory of Lud and here there are three ancient burial mounds and a well all in a line. Dowsing rods readily showed this was an energy line - a dragon line. Just by is a place called Frog Hole and this may, indeed, refer to the amphibian creature but it may also refer to the Old Woman, the

Luds Well on the way to Pilsbury - a shrine to the Celtic god.

Hag or the Earth Mother, *Language of the Goddess* Marija Gimbutas, Thames and Hudson and was often portrayed as a frog with a vulva on her back. This is a goddess of birth and of regeneration. She is also sometimes shown as a toad or a serpent.

Our first trip to the Well of Lud was eventful to say the least. We stopped at Hartington, and then took the car along the gated track. We parked on the grass at the side of the road and strolled towards Lud's Well and enjoyed the area for what it was - a delight. The lark was in full voice as it fluttered skywards and it stopped its sweet song as it descended. An angler was pitting his wits against the brown trout - the brownies - in the waters to the west of the track and the black and white cattle were drinking the sweet flowing liquid. All was well with the world until a group of about forty something cyclists, mountain bikers, careered down the road and realised there was a closed gate in front of them. Screech, bang, crash. Some of them were in a heap, some of the tail enders shouted. Thankfully none were badly hurt - although some were suffering from hurt pride - and on they went with a chorus of agitated voices.

It was as we inspected the Well that the Dark Side manifested itself and, perhaps, was defeated by the Shining One. To explain (and deviate) it is necessary to tell of an experience neither I nor Hilary would wish on anyone. It was an experience brought about by evil thoughts from a misguided person or persons and it is the very nature of this that people in the past have interpreted as dark and satanic - Black Magic or Satanism. I would not give this experience the credence it desires, but I relate the story as a warning to others that the power of the mind can be very, very strong indeed. Especially when misused. It has been the same throughout history, when the Evil Eye has been placed on people because they would not do this that or the other, or for any reason whatsoever.

The story must start before our visit to the Well. I am not

117

The waters that flow from Luds Well - out of the limestone hillside to the East and into the sour landscape to the West. This is where the Earth Mother's milk once sweetened the ground and where her companion, Lud, reigned.

118

going to identify the people involved. They know who they are but they may not be aware of what they caused. Suffice to say that as a result of a request they made to me connected with a business proposition - which I innocently and politely turned down - our previously good relationship ended. It must be said that neither Hilary nor I wished it that way and indeed, the way it manifested itself came as a complete shock to the both of us but it is now obvious that the rejection of their business proposition affected them, or one of them, greatly. It was something that could never have worked, and I turned them down in (I thought) a pleasant enough way with a "thanks very much." But the Evil Eye looked on us. They are both very psychic people and have powerful minds and it is possible that the black thoughts sent our way emanated from their subconscious. Consciously they may not have been aware of what they were causing at all, and what powers they were sending our way, but it soon became obvious that strong forces were affecting us. The best way we could fend them off, we felt, was to return loving thoughts and this we did. But the dark side still loomed. I had one or two near misses whilst driving my car. Hilary's car repeatedly cut out and inspection of the engine showed that the petrol pipe had a leak that resulted in a fountain of petrol cascading onto the engine block. Had the engine not have cut out as it did the machine would have got hotter and hotter and the consequence of a fountain of petrol pouring on a hot engine is unthinkable. We like to think someone was watching over us (and, in fact, we know exactly who it was). There were other, similar, occurrences until we travelled that day to Hartington and the Celtic well.

As a result of these unpleasant occurrences we were informing, and probably boring, as many people as possible about what was happening. Many were full of good advice and one of our cherished friends went to a great deal of trouble and performed an act of ceremonial magic and presented an amulet to ward off the Evil Eye.

As Hilary walked along the well worn path to the mouth of the well that particular day - a Sunday - the waters were cascading forth from the limestone hillside into the gritstone valley - sweet water pouring on to sour ground. It was then that she was lifted into the air and dropped to the floor.

By what, it is impossible to say and, thank goodness, she was not hurt. Shocked she most certainly was for it is not exactly an everyday happening. She picked herself up and dusted herself down. And that was that.

What exactly had she experienced? Was it a continuation of the bad events that we both had experienced or was it a fight between good and evil that she found herself in the middle of? Who can say. If, indeed, it was a clash of good and bad, then who was doing the fighting? Was it the powerful goodly thoughts we had been sending competing against the powerful black thoughts coming our way? Was our friend's ritual and the amulet doing the job? Or was it Lud, the Shining One, putting in his four pennyworth?

It was not only the ancient Celts, and their ancestors who still live today in Ireland, Wales (and parts of Derbyshire) who believe in the doctrine of the power of 'demons' in the lives of people. The early and medieval Christians did likewise. Both religions believed in the miraculous healing of diseases and afflictions. The Jewish doctrines also told of 'possession by devils' and Jesus cured by casting out devils. These 'devils' or 'demons', were often cast out by people who knew of the powers of the mind, and the powers of the earth - people who were sometimes referred to as Wise Men or Wise Women - and here I would refer you to my own great aunt whom I mention in *Staffordshire: its Magic and Mystery*. Sometimes these people were also called Witches and sometimes they were killed or tortured for what they did. We have all experienced 'black dogs' on our shoulders, the black moods we find ourselves in. These are a manifestation of the mind and are best cured by another manifestation of the mind.

Returning to the Well of Lud, I wonder whether it was worshipped for the healing properties it contained? It is most likely, especially because of the minerals it contained having sprung from a limestone base, and I wonder whether it is still giving healing. I think it is. For I think both Hilary and I were cured of that intended affliction of the Evil Eye during the visit.

Returning to the car we had parked on the verge - please DO park carefully and wisely, for the road is only wide enough for one car and if you are not parked fully off the carriageway then passing vehicles, especially milk trucks, have to drive on to the field and a tumble down to the waters below has not been unknown.

We had the good fortune of meeting the farmer from Ludwell Farm. He told us how the waters from the well were the finest around until a while back when pot holers decided to go down into its depths. They removed some of the stones that surrounded it and, he said, the water has never been the same. It is now, officially, not drinkable but he has lived there all his life and has drunk of it for countless years and is a very healthy looking elderly gentleman. He has thrived on it. Just what those potholers changed by moving those stones at the mouth we may now never know. I asked him if he knew why it was named Lud Well and he confessed he did not, although his wife had always thought it was because it made a "Loud" sound. Lud was also known as the Loud

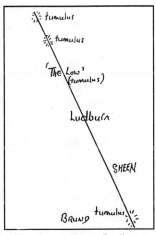

The dragon line at Ludburn.

One.

There are wells by the hundreds and thousands in and around our three Counties and many of them are simply supplies of water, dug to bring liquid from the ground. Others are more than that, they are something special. Today, especially in Derbyshire, many sources of water are decorated and used as bait for the tourists. Well Dressings are not only colourful, they are delightful and I would not knock this revived custom at all, but I feel we should be aware that what takes place now is a modern day idea of how sources of water from Mother Earth used to be worshipped in Celtic pagan times. Later, the Puritans put a stop to statues being placed at 'holy' wells and they put a stop to sacrifices; by then the ritual human sacrifice had undoubtedly ended, but there were sacrifices of personal belongings and of animals. We still throw money into wells for the goddess to grant a wish and today the Anglican Church has taken over the ceremonies.

Place of Pilgrimage

The Spa Town of Buxton, for instance, one of the most civilised spots in the Universe according to some, is a place founded because of the magical properties of its healing waters. Most of us are aware of the main well from which the warm water flows and to which many flock, but picture, if you will, the town in 'olden' times, way before the grand hotels and shops were thought of. Then, it was a place of pilgrimage acknowledged not only by the Romans but by people alive long before their invasion. They came to the grove in the valley from where the warm waters flowed from the ground - is it such a coincidence that one of the local pubs in the vicinity is called The Grove? - and they came to be healed. Many still come to the town to be healed. What an awe-inspiring sight it must have been for the traveller approaching the Buxton valley. It would have been covered in trees, possibly oaks and ash and yew, and the warmish water would have turned to mist as it touched the colder air. This mist blanket must have been hovering over this sacred site for months on end.

It was not just to the one well that the pilgrims flocked. There were many springs oozing their mineral-rich liquid. Some have now disappeared and others are still in evidence. I had the pleasure of visiting one of these 'hidden gems' early in 1995 when I and a few members of the Green Dragon Mysteries Society were invited by Beryl Thompson, the leading light of the Buxton Psychic Group, to see what is now known as the Beggars' Well or Paupers' Bath (among other names). It stands at the rear of the Old Hall Hotel and, really, nothing could be seen of it because it was boarded up. In Victorian times this was a well where the poor could bathe free of charge and there is little or no written evidence of it being in use earlier than that.

This is where I am at odds with local historians because their training tells them that if there is no documentation then there is no proof; therefore this well was not in use before the Victorians because there is nothing written down suggesting its use. I use my heart, my head and my dowsing rods. My heart told me that this spot felt right and was a place of healing. My head said that if the warm waters

The site of the neglected healing well at Buxton.

flowed from the ground then it would not have been ignored over the centuries until the Victorians decided to use it and my dowsing rods said there was an earth energy line going through the spot, adding that certain 'zest' to the waters. Beryl and friends want the well to be used for healing again and, at the time of writing, there are moves afoot to restore it. I hope they succeed.

Rites of Fertility

Like the well dressing ceremonies, many of our ancient customs have been revived but are now a pale shadow of their former selves. Ceremonies at the wells involved much merrymaking, mirth and sexual encounter. Not only was the goddess being observed but life and the continuation of life was being recognised. Most May Day ceremonies acknowledged the end of a long winter and the beginning of a, hopefully, good summer. It was - and still is - a time when the sap stirs and the Rites of Spring come to the fore. Young maidens cavorted around a huge phallic symbol - the Maypole - and lasses and lads took leave of their dads and away to the maypole high.

The Commonwealth of Oliver Cromwell put a stop to most of this fun and frolic, or at least they put a stop to it where they knew it was going on. When Charles II was restored to the throne people could have fun again and the restoration was celebrated with Oakapple Day, May 29th. Many of the old May Day fertility rites were restored, but disguised under the banner of Oakapple Day (so named because of the tradition that the King hid in an oak tree, hence the 'Royal Oak' pub signs). The ancient pagan fertility rites reared their heads again, and one such place that has kept the tradition very much alive is Castleton, a little way from Buxton.

Today, many hundreds of tourists flock to see the horse rider dressed in Stuart costume have a huge garland of flowers placed over his head and then parade around the village. All very quaint, but lurking underneath this ceremony are quite a few relics of the Old Ways. The ceremony actually commences the previous day when oak (the sacred tree of the Celtic Druids) and other foliage is fastened around the pinnacles of the church tower. At the same time flowers are gathered. These used to be mainly wild flowers but times have changed and many attractive cultivated specimens can be found within the garland. They are tied up in bunches and placed onto a beehive-shaped frame some three feet tall, or thereabouts. When completed it can weigh well over half a hundredweight. Then a special 'posy' is made up and placed at the top of the garland. This is called the 'Queen' and used to signify the maidenhead, although this connotation has now been forgotten or hidden.

On the day itself, the King and his Consort - both riding fine horses - parade around the boundary of the village. These horses used to be white, again a relic of the Celtic traditions for white horses which featured prominently in their beliefs, and the female Consort used to be a man dressed as a woman. This is not unusual in ancient rites by any stretch of the imagination. Later in this book we shall be looking at the Alderley Mummers and a tradition of many Mummers or Soulers is the Male/Female She-Male. I have referred to this in a book, *Cheshire: Its Magic and Mystery*, when I visited the Antrobus Soulers. And at Abbotts Bromley in Staffordshire (*Staffordshire: its Magic and Mystery*) there is still the Horn Dance when one of the main characters is a man dressed as woman. This is not done in a blatant sexual sense of transvestism, it is more like a pantomime dame, a comical character, and I think this is the origin, in fact, of the pantomime dames we know today. They signify the duality and are the symbol of fertility, Mother Earth if you like.

As the King and his Consort (the man was ousted by a woman in 1955) ride the village boundaries the garland or beehive

125

is paraded on a pole to whichever public house has been designated the 'host' for that year. The huge garland is hoisted over the King's head and sits on his shoulders and the parade begins again. This time the King and Consort have a brass band following and also a number of young schoolgirls, all bedecked in white and carrying small maypole symbols. This is, like it or not, a throwback to the blatant sexual days of yore. The white signifies the girls are maidens or virgins and the maypole is, or rather used to be, a phallic symbol. It is certainly not viewed that way today. The procession stops outside each of the village's six pubs - another throwback to the old days of much revelry - and the landlord brings out ale and mineral water. This procession takes in the region of two hours and during the pub stops, the girls dance a special dance, called the 'circle and chain'.

On arrival at the Market Place the girls dance six dances around a Maypole proper. During this, the King and Consort ride to the churchyard and onto the base of the church tower. The 'Queen' is removed from the garland and the garland is then hoisted from the King's shoulders and lifted up to the top of the tower where it remains for a week. Nowadays, the 'Queen' is placed on the war memorial, a tribute to the fallen. Earlier it was with the garland and, whereas the church has now taken over the ceremony, the garland and the 'queen' used to have other ceremonial purposes with the maypole. A tradition has it that, once, a local vicar threw the garland down from the tower because the ceremony was, he thought, pagan. He was correct in his thinking but the church has long had a policy of adopting an "if you can't beat 'em, join 'em, policy" and adopted old beliefs as their own. After all, most of the old churches are built on sites of Earth Worship and some of the ways of old are still depicted around churches.

There are many theories about what the garland day actually

stands for. Most agree that it is to do with fertility - the time of celebration used to be known locally as Baby Night for it was when so many of the villagers were conceived - and one idea has it that the flowers in the garland were a sacrifice to ensure crops grew later in the year. Another is that the garland, a huge head, denotes the Celtic Cult of the Head for it was believed the spirit of a person resided in his head. A captured enemy always had his head lopped off and displayed on a pole in those days of the Celts.

The Consort - until 1955 it was a man dressed as a woman, a She-Male common throughout England.

The Celtic Cult of the Head was still prominent in Saxon times for there are Saxon carved stone heads displayed in the entrance porch to Bakewell Church. Many stone heads used to be displayed at wells within Staffordshire, Cheshire and Derbyshire. If they were not removed by the church authorities they were removed by people eager to use them as garden or house ornaments. I have come across a number in front gardens and often wonder what stories they could tell.

The Castleton church tower decorated with memories of the past.

Another Derbyshire celebration: Chapel en le Frith Carnival, 1947. Many such events throughout the Three Shires have origins going back a long way and many celebrated the Rites of Spring and Summer. *(courtesy Buxton Advertiser)*

The King, his horse and the garland: a huge head of flowers.
Above: when decorated and **below:** before the ceremony. *T Matthews*

Saint George defeats the Dragon again

It was Samhain of 1993 - All Hallows Eve, or Halloween - when Hilary and I had the pleasure of travelling the lanes of mid Cheshire with the Antrobus Soulers, a fine band of men who have kept alive the tradition of Souling or, as some would have it, Mumming, for many a day. I waxed lyrical about their performance and went into great detail about their traditions and what they represented and were all about in *"Cheshire: its Magic and Mystery"*. That book came out in the winter of 1994 and after it had hit the bookshelves I received a telephone call.

"What about us?" a voice on the other end asked, "We have revived the ancient Alderley Mummers and there's not a mention of that." The caller was friendly and I was invited to the first of their winter performances at the Dog and Partridge pub in Bollington Cross, just north of Macclesfield.

It was just before Christmas when the Alderley Mummers were due to appear at the 'Dog' and we were looking forward to what was to come, for it had become apparent that these chaps, who used to be the Adlington Morris Men, were not only very well up on local folk traditions but we both knew some of them. And the beer was good at the 'Dog' so what more could we ask? A roaring fire would not go amiss on that particular night, we both thought, and we were not disappointed. The blazing log fire had not been laid on for our benefit but it might as well have been, for we were mightily cold on that Winter's evening. Anyway, the cold was soon forgotten and a warm evening was had by all. The leading light of the revived Alderley Mummers is a fine chap by the name of Duncan Broomhead and on that particular night poor Duncan was suffering from a rotten bout of the 'flu. He was in his sick bed but made the effort to come to Bollington from his home in Cheadle Hulme. I will be forever grateful to him. However, it was soon clear that he was in no fit state to have a chat so he was sent back to bed and we arranged to meet later, when the Mummers were due to perform their ancient ceremonial play at the Wild Boar up in the hills above Macclesfield.

It was then that I was filled in with the whys and the wherefores of that particular band of merry men. The traditional play they now perform is the one that tenants of the Stanley Estate in Alderley or, more correctly, Nether Alderley, used to put on for the Lord of the Manor and his family and friends at Christmas. The words had been collected from Alec Barber, late of Nether Alderley and later of Broken Cross at Macclesfield, and costume details were from Fred Barber of Lyme Green. Additional text was from the personal notes of Clem Barber (and here I think it is needless to point out that the Barber family were the mainstays of the Alderley Mummers for many, many years).

This play, I was informed, was performed regularly at Christmas and New Year up to 1937 by members of the Barber family, who were tenants of the Stanleys. It had originally been performed in the farmhouses of the estate but latterly it was presented in the Tenants Hall as part of the Christmas festivities. This change in time of appearance, according to a transcript of the play I was very kindly presented with, seems to have dated from about 1900 when the play was revived after a lapse of twenty years. Soon after the 1937 performance the Stanley Estate was broken up and sold and the performance lapsed as the tenants were scattered. It features many characters familiar to the Souling or Mumming plays in various other parts of the country, especially in Cheshire. There is St George, the Enter-in (sometimes the Letter-in), Prince Paradise (sometimes the Black Prince), the Doctor, Colonel Slasher, Beelzebub, the Groom and Young Ball, the horse. This character has a real horse's skull covered in black material and attached to a pole and is carried by a man covered with a black cloth. I noticed that the performance differs somewhat from others I have seen in that it does

131

not possess one of the characters we have alluded to previously - the she-male or the man dressed as a woman. I suspect that the character was considered not suitable for a performance in front of the Lord of the Manor and his family. This could have stemmed either from the Stanley family members themselves or by the performers of the old play, I know not which - although I could, of course, be mistaken. However, this character, which is symbolic of fertility and rebirth (just as the figure used to be at Castleton), is important. The present Alderley Mummers are absolutely right in sticking to the play as they have been given it and should not change it at all, but I feel we should be aware of the missing character. Apart from the she-male's non appearance the play is almost identical to all the others even to the fact that the horse is made from a real horse's head. This, of course, stretches back to Celtic times, as we have seen before, and the Cult of the Head. I also believe that the play, performed for the Stanleys at Christmas, would have been performed at All Hallows Eve a long time ago and that the date was changed to please the Lord and Master.

The present day Alderley Mummers are a grand body of men who have kept alive the traditions of the past just as their forerunners, the Mummers of old, did in days long gone. Some of the costumes they wear today have been handed down to them by the Barbers and some have been made anew, copied from old photographs supplied by the Barber family. The traditions behind the performance stretch back way before the Conqueror came to these shores and much of what is now said and acted is lost on modern day audiences, but their appearance in a pub at Christmastime does much to enrich life for everyone who has the privilege of seeing them.

Both I and Hilary have no hesitation in thanking the present-day Alderley Mummers for their hospitality and friendliness and for their enthusiasm and, judging by their reception we have witnessed in local hostelries, a lot more people thank them as well. They have done far more than most to retain the old values and traditions. Well done, lads!

MUMMERS BACK TO LIFE.

CENTURY OLD PLAY AT MANSION.

QUAINT SCENES.

FROM OUR OWN REPORTER.

Alderley Park, Cheshire, Tuesday.

"My Lord, the mummers."

LORD STANLEY OF ALDERLEY nodded genially as he sat to-night in the hall of ancient Alderley Park, surrounded by his guests, his tenants, and their children.

A towering Christmas tree, bereft of its presents, stood in one corner; the children, flushed from "Gathering peascods," stood as far away as possible from a roaring log fire in the grate.

It was a scene that has been unchanged each New Year's Eve for 127 years, and somehow, as the staff of the leading mummer rattled on the oaken door, one almost expected to see once more billowing frills and tight trousers, flickering candles, and the clatter of hoofs.

THE BARBER FAMILY.

It was the Barber family of Alderley who first presented the mummers' play before the lord and lady of the manor, and to-night, as at each annual performance, every one of the eight "actors" bore the name of Barber.

An extract from a 1929 newspaper.
Courtesy of Duncan Broomhead.

Beelzebub at Alderley

The Barber family perform the Mumming Play for the Lord of the Manor
some time in the 1920s or 30s.   *Courtesy of Duncan Broomhead.*

Prince Paradise, another of the
Alderley Mummers. In parts of
Cheshire and Staffordshire he is
known as the Black Prince.

Colonel Slasher in full voice at the Wild
Boar Inn, during the Yuletide perambulations
of the Alderley Mummers.

8
SUN AND MOON WORSHIP

Andrew Collins is an Essex man and, on the surface, has nothing to do with this neck of the woods. His southern accent sticks out a mile against the rounded tones of the Three Shires and his looks certainly set him apart as well. His brown hair flows down his spine to his backside and his small and round dark glasses perched on the end of his nose are, ever so slightly, unusual. But Andrew, or Andy as I call him, has his heart placed firmly here. He is a friendly soul and gets on with most people and he keeps returning and returning to this place he loves so deeply.

He is in point of fact, one of the most celebrated authors in his own field of Earth Mysteries or New Age writing. He and his companion Graham Phillips developed what they term Psychic Questing and they both have a considerable following. They are both internationally renowned.

Andy was guest speaker at the midsummer meeting of the Green Dragon Mysteries Society and after he had shown slides and given an outline of what Psychic Questing was all about he and some fifty or so others trotted off to, hopefully, witness the Double Sunset - the unique event experienced only at Leek - but it was not to be. The sun set behind Bosley Cloud and, instead of re-appearing to the right as it should at this time of the year, it vanished from sight, save for a faint white glow. No-one was surprised for it is very rare these days to be able to see this mystical double sunset. At one time it was a matter-of-fact annual event but either a slight tilt in the Earth's axis, or a 'wobble' or different air pollution or whatever, has meant it has not been seen for many a year. Technically, it is the obliquity of the ecliptic causing a change - a fact mentioned in the 1800s Official Guide to the North Staffs Railway: *"the sun's great northern declination may be gradually adjusted and at length perhaps limited"*.

The following morning Andy was due to return to Essex but after his breakfast at the bed and breakfast establishment where he had stayed for the night he telephoned me and we both decided to visit Lud Church. He had read about Lud Church and had mentioned it in a couple of his books, *The Circlemakers* and *The Seventh Sword,* and was fascinated. He wanted to take this opportunity of actually seeing it again. So off we went. The morning was delightful. The midsummer sun was shining brightly and a cloudless sky meant temperatures were into the 80s. We certainly made the most of it, and our walk along the River Dane and into Back Forest took longer than it should because we both wanted to savour the idyllic summer's morn.

I have mentioned before about the amulets that have been made from clay or mud found at Lud Church and all around the Roaches and Andy had a theory concerning orgone energy - special properties contained in the rocks and the earth around ancient mystical sites. We discussed this as we walked along and I warned him that, although the weather was hot it would still be cool inside the cavernous natural cleft. There was hardly ever any sun shining in there, I warned. But how wrong I was.

When we arrived and entered the 'Green Chapel', the sun was high in the sky. It was mid day at mid summer and the golden orb's rays illuminated and warmed the cavern. It was the only time I have ever witnessed the sun shining into Lud Church and I have visited the spot on numerous occasions. It is usually a notoriously bad place to photograph because of the lack of natural lighting but this day was different. It could not have been better and Andy used a whole roll of film inside a few minutes. He certainly made the most of it and I wished I had brought my camera as well but I did persuade him to let me have some copies of the ones he took.

"The Sun God is certainly looking down on us today!" said Andy, and I agreed. After he had had a good look round and taken all the pictures he could we both agreed it would be good to 'tune in' to the spot and to do a bit of 'psychic questing' while we were here.

I sat on a rock in the middle of the vast natural 'chapel' used by so many different people for so many different reasons over so many centuries, and Andy stood beside me. He is a natural psychic and medium, and I have been able to develop my own skills to a degree over the years and we both began our own meditation, before raising a 'cone of energy'. Anyone entering Lud Church at that time could have been forgiven for wanting to turn back in a hurry if they had witnessed the pair of us. Andy's voice echoed and accentuated as he began to talk us through the 'ceremony' of creating a cone of energy and requesting Guardians of the Place to assist us.

We began with breathing exercises and then imagined a powerful light which we took in through our nostrils and into our bodies. This light filled our bodies and came out through our auras, cascading to the ground and swirling in a clockwise direction until a wheel of light was formed. It then became a solid floor of light and rose up around us, joining above our heads in a beehive shape and then emitting sparks and spots like a revolving dance hall light does. Our Cone of Psychic Energy was now around us and Andy called out to any Guardians of the Place who wished to help or join us to please do so, if they so desired. He also called for any of our own Spirit Guides or Helpers to join if they, too, so wished. The air around me was electric, I could feel the force we had created; it was like static electricity but the whole place was quiet and peaceful apart from the sound of birdsong.

We both remained quiet and contemplative for a few minutes and then I noticed a hare - real or imaginary I could not say -

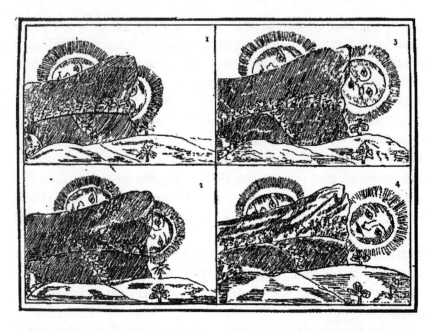

A rather unusual view of the Double Sunset, taken from an old book Miller's History of Leek. It shows the sun setting behind Bosley Cloud (fig.1) and seeming to move (fig.2) until it finally emerges again from the side of the Cloud, but not yet set below the horizon (fig.4).

There has been much quarrying at the Cloud over the years, and if this illustration indeed reflects how the hill used to look then it is easy to notice that the shape has now changed. Certainly, stone was used from it to construct both the nearby canal and also used for foundations of the railway viaduct in the valley below. It was probably at this time that an unusual natural rock formation, a huge corkscrew-like structure, was demolished. It was known as Bully Thrumble.

The Leek Times, week ending July 18th, 1884, wrote:

'The phenomena for which Leek is famous, namely the double setting of the sun as seen in the old churchyard, was eagerly watched for this year; but except on the evening of the 18th every sunset was obscured. In olden days before the rock called Bully Thrumble on the crest of the Cloud was blasted down, and before the fir trees on the ridge beyond Packsaddle Hollow took off somewhat of the lower height of the hill, the double sunsets must have been glorious sights. We believe that the phenomena may still be seen from Leek Moor for a few nights longer.'

138

which came along the cavern floor, went by the two of us and hopped towards one of the high walls. The hare turned silver and became inanimate and a silver crescent moon appeared above it. What looked to me like a cross or a key appeared below it and the three objects, the moon, the hare and the key, hovered in the air. I found out afterwards that Andy had also seen the crescent moon and the key but not the hare. He had seen a curiously shaped rock like nothing he had witnessed anywhere else. He described it as being monolithic but its top was flat and sloping. He had also seen a male figure in a green tunic, a sort of Robin Hood type which he interpreted as the Green Man. He got the impression that this strange rock was part of the ritualistic aspect of the area as a whole and was connected with Sun and Moon worship. We reversed the cone of energy, reducing it and finally removing it from our bodies, thanked those who had helped, and we came back to 'reality'. After we had both compared what we had 'seen' I instantly recognised the strangely shaped rock Andy had been shown. It was Hanging Stone.

I have described it before as an 'awesome and menacing rock structure' and there are many legends connected with this formation of rocks, not least of human sacrifices. It is less than a mile from Lud Church and I know that Andy was not aware of its existence. We walked to it and as soon as he saw the imposing structure he gave a shout of delight.

"That's it, that's the rock I saw" he said and we clambered up the steep path to it.

The views from Hanging Stone are wonderful and as awe-inspiring as the stone itself. To the west is Bosley Cloud and to the South is Gun Hill. To the East the whole range of the Roaches stretch out and down below, in the valley, the Dane runs its cheery way.

We both thought it was time for another bit of 'questing' and we settled ourselves down beside Hanging Stone. I was again visited by the hare and by the crescent moon while Andy saw the crescent moon rising and falling over Gun Hill. He also saw monk-like figures and a round building with a thatched roof that he associated with corn, possibly a storage place for corn. He got the distinct impression that it was from Hanging Stone that a phenomena associated with the moon could be witnessed at a certain point in the year, just like

Hanging Stone, Swythamley

the Double Sunset. The hare is often associated with the moon and it is also associated with corn. It is depicted as the moon god and was regarded as a symbol of fertility and Spring. It was revered as the Spirit of the Corn and reaping of the last of the corn was known as 'cutting the hare'. And as for the monk-like figure? We were standing, or rather sitting, at a spot that was once part of a Grange of a Cistercian Abbey.

Lud Church was illuminated at mid summer, and it is perhaps the only time of year when the entire cavern is greeted by the Sun God. There were distinct clues for us about Moon Worship and perhaps the entire area was used for both Sun and Moon ceremonies. Couple this with the Double Sunset at Leek and the moon phenomenon and we may be able to begin to appreciate what the whole of the landscape was about. The natural cycle of death and rebirth, brought out in the saga Gawain and the Green Knight set at Swythamley, Lud Church and the Roaches, is there for us to see if we but could. Perhaps we should not be looking at these spots individually but collectively. I think that is what we were being told as we looked out over Gun Hill that morning at midsummer - and the Quest should continue. Neither of us wanted to move away from that spot, but Andy had to begin his travels South, although we both agreed a few more minutes wouldn't make much difference.

"What's that hill called?" Andy asked as we looked over at Gun Hill. It was there that he felt the moon could be seen to rise and fall in a certain way at a certain date and he wondered whether its name implied anything to do with the moon. I told him it was Gun Hill and told him of the legends associated with it:

We were also looking down upon a farm known as Old Hag. It was here that a legend sprung up about an old woman, a hag, who many thought of as a witch. She would be paid to turn herself into a hare so that the hunter could have sport and chase her and use his shooting prowess. One day he shot the hare in the leg and later the old woman was found lying behind a wall, shot in the leg. This entire area holds many mysteries. I have mentioned a circle of stones discovered at nearby Bartomley Farm and possibly a solar or lunar alignment; there is an ancient stone cross in the grounds of Swythamley Hall and the valley is supposed, according to local legend, to have been the site of a ferocious battle countless centuries ago. A hoard of Roman treasure was found in a Neolithic burial mound in the land owned by Bartomley Farm and included a gold mask thought to denote, most interestingly, the Roman Sun God.

As we left the site, Andy re-emphasised to me his feelings concerning this rock outcrop having been a lunar observatory connected in some way with the solar-oriented Lud Church and the Double Setting Sun phenomenon at nearby Leek. He later wrote: *"Somehow they appeared to form individual components of a much larger picture involving an intimate knowledge of geo-*

celestial events and a long lost ceremonial landscape of great age."

I had expected to leave this whole question of the Sun and Moon connections in this Land of the Green Knight right there at that point until I either got a computer print-out - which in all probability would have made my brain itch, anyway - or I and others went there again. I had filed away in my mind the thought that I would like to bring Hilary with me to that spot one day, for her psychic talents could very well help the Quest considerably, but had done no more - and then I received a phone call from Andy Collins. He had talked to a number of people about our psychic experience when he returned to Essex and rang to tell me where he was up to. His familiar southern tones were on the other end of the line

"Hi!" said Andy. "I've been doing a bit of research and asking a few questions since I got home. First of all, about the Double Sunset. It seems quite likely that a change in the shift of the Earth might very well have affected the actual day on which the Sunset can now been seen. It could be a few days either way."

He explained a bit more about the 'axial wobble' and obliquity of the ecliptic and then turned his attention to the Lunar cycles. "I've been consulting the experts" he said. "There's been lots of work done on this, particularly in regards to standing stones and other sites in Scotland. Apparently, there's a phenomena known as the Lunar Standstill Cycle. It's a bit like the Solar Cycle when the Midsummer Sun could be seen from Leek to rise and set. The Lunar Cycle occurs every 18.6 years and the last one was in 1987, and it's when the moon rises, slants over in an arc and goes down again - due south. As though it comes straight up then goes straight down. That's about it - the next time we'll be able to witness it is a few years away yet!" It is visible more or less due south in the sky, and that is the direction from Hanging Stone looking towards Gun.

Some days after Andy's return home, a package arrived in the post for me. It was from Essex and it contained a word-processed document entitled *New insight into the celestial alignments of the Staffordshire Moorlands - an intuitive perspective*. Part of it reads:

> It was not until 10 days after my visit to the Staffordshire Moorlands with Doug Pickford that I had a chance to check the lunar standstill cycle to see how, if at all, it might fit into the picture. Speaking to astronomer and electronics engineer Rodney Hale about the low arc I had seen the moon conduct over the southerly-positioned Gun Hill, he informed me that this is indeed what happens at the end of the moon's 18.66 year cycle. Fired by his words I searched through my collection of occasional papers and founded the 'Moonwatch Supplement' put out by the Ley Hunter magazine to coincide with the end of the last lunar standstill in 1987.

> In an article entitled *Castlerigg* by John Glover and R D Y Perrett it outlined the nature of the lunar standstill and I was stunned by what I found. The two most significant times in this special lunar year are the nights when the course of the moon makes low arcs over the southern horizon - the so-called Most Southerly Rising Moon (MSRM) - and over the northern horizon - the Most Northerly Rising Moon (MNRM). The last mentioned phenomenon occurs during December, while the Most Southerly Rising Moon - what I had presumably seen in mind whilst at the Hanging Stone - takes place around midsummer and is known as the Midsummer Major Standstill Moon.

> I am now certain that what I watched in mind was the Midsummer Major Standstill Moon rising and setting over Gun Hill at some point in the distant past, perhaps even in Neolithic times. The fact that this ritual landscape seems to embody the potency of the midsummer cycle in its alignments and traditions seems to bear out this supposition, and explains why my mind should have connected Lud Church with the Hanging Stone rock formation.

If the theory suggested by our miniature Psychic Quest is correct - that the whole area was not just devoted to Sun Worship as in the mystical Double Sunset visible from Leek but had Moon connections with the Lunar Standstill - then this land has been one of the 'holiest' there could be in the eyes of those who have gone before. Forget Glastonbury, forget Avebury and the rest. Here, in the Mystical Middle of England, is one of the most magical and mystical sites there has ever been.

No wonder a considerable number of writers and researchers have been led to this area and no wonder it gets in your blood. Two such natural happenings within such a small area would have been a considerable source of wonder and awe, and with other phenomena including Lud's Church, Bosley Cloud, Shining Tor, Shutlingslow, the Bawdstone and others it can be no surprise that pilgrims, poets, anchorites and priests, royalty and Wise People have been drawn like magnets. Neither is it a surprise that they still are.

Gun Hill, seen from Hanging Stone.

Was Hanging Stone once an observatory from where the Lunar Rise and Fall could be witnessed? The entire area around here - from Leek (Double Sunset) to the Roaches (Spring and Autumn equinox observations from the Bawdstone Healing Rock) to Lud Church (a solar temple the sun illuminates at midsummer) - could have been a vast Ceremonial Landscape. It would explain a lot - from why a mask of the Sun God was discovered at a farm in Wincle to why psychics and mystics are still drawn to this area. It has been pointed out (*Leek - the other Silbury Hill? Linda Skellam, Three Shires Mysteries Magazine, Summer 1995*) that the Double Sunset is the opposite to the mystical Double Sunrise viewed from Silbury Hill.

9
HAUNTINGS AND HAPPENINGS

I have mentioned ghosts, phantoms and spirits many times before in many books. They are part of ourselves, our landscapes and our buildings. They are parts of our very souls. As we journey towards the conclusion of this book, I would like to mention just a few more. There are many that I could have drawn attention to - we all have our own personal ghosts - but the ones I relate are very telling happenings. Conclusions there may be, and then again maybe not. If there are, those conclusions must be yours. This first story has never been chronicled before. I was contacted by the gentleman who experienced the strange phenomena I shall tell of, and I visited him on three or four occasions and found him to be lucid and highly intelligent.

Colin Jones used to be a real 'Jack the Lad' - a man who loved women and drink. Today he is not only a happy family man, he is a person who sings the praises of Christ. The shelves in the study of his beautiful 250 year old residence 'Rosedale' just off the Macclesfield to Leek road at Bosley are lined with theological works and he has been a regular attender at Bible Study Classes and at Christian Fellowships. A far cry indeed from the life he used to lead.

The conversion was a rapid one, brought on by an evil presence in his home and by an exorcism carried out by the then local Vicar. The story Colin tells shows not only his immense bravery against an unseen force but also vividly portrays the lurking Powers of Darkness.

It began on Boxing Day of 1983 and continued until the New Year. It was a sunny day, unusual for the time of year, and the lady who was living with Colin at that time was not feeling very well and went for a lie down on the bed. Colin went upstairs and asked

145

if he could do anything for her and she asked for an orange juice. He went down the stairs to get it and as he did so he heard a bump. The old house was always alive with creaks in the floorboards and tappings in the radiator pipes and they had both made jokes about it and, as he heard the noise, Colin made light of it.

He returned to the landing and decided to open two windows to let some air in and as he did so saw that a vase had blown over. As he went to pick the vase up he was thrown into the air, across the landing and into the bedroom - a distance of some twenty feet. He landed on the floor and felt what he described as 'a force' holding him down. He told me: "I fought with it and I fought very strongly. I struggled to get her off the bed - her hair stood up and her face looked like she was going very fast on a motorcycle. Her skin was pulled back and tight - and then we went into the landing and down the stairs. It was like going through treacle".

They left the house and went to friends at Whitely Green. He telephoned an electrician and asked him to inspect the house, which was done in rapid time, and he reported that nothing was wrong with the electrics. Colin even went for a full medical examination with BUPA and there was nothing untoward. He continued: "There was only one thing for it. We were going back to the house. Me, her, a Doberman dog and no clothes !"

They walked through the door and noticed a depression had settled over the house. "The air seemed to be thick," was how Colin described it, but they decided to remain. Colin is something of a tenacious character and will not let anything get the better of him and he decided to go and see the previous occupant who told him he had seen a "Victorian gent" in what used to be the workshop by the side of the house. When Colin took a look around that area he found a Ouija Board tucked away. In an effort to find an answer to what had taken place - and why it had taken place - he visited the people who lived at Rosedale before that and the people who were occupants before that.

His story then moves to New Year's Day and Colin decided to walk his dog around the nearby reservoir early in the morning. He returned to the house at about 8am and went into the kitchen. The lady he was living with was in bed. He took off his wet clothes and plugged in the kettle which promptly "sailed up the room" and smashed. On previous occasions his ladyfriend had witnessed the kettle move as if of its own accord. Said Colin: "The air went thick and I heard a noise like a whooshing sound - rather like a train coming in from a distance and then going past - and my hair stood up on end with total fear. The mirror on the wall turned round. I went outside and sat down, totally fearful of going back in. The Doberman hit the decks and would not move. It was then that I got thinking and I became thoroughly angry and went inside. I went upstairs and said 'Do you mind making a cup of tea - we've a visitor." I didn't actually tell her what I had experienced but she came down and flew out of the house - she had heard the noise and her hair went up just like mine and she ran, almost totally naked, up the road. I ran after her and got her back and we sat down in the lounge. There was fear and hatred all around us. There was also a slight smell. we decided to go shopping to get out of the place and came back later."

A week went by during which nothing happened but there was a feeling of depression; then a noise, like the one heard before but also described as a 'drumming, getting faster as it got nearer' was heard. Colin described it as like a train in the distance but as it got closer it became like a drumbeat. They managed to get through that 'happening' and, occasionally, the noise would come again. "We were still frightened, but not to the same extent," he said. The two were able to talk about it more than they had previously.

As the New Year progressed, snow began to fall and Colin

was in his car at North Rode. He been forced to make some detours because of the weather and he heard that noise and saw the silhouette of a figure sitting next to him in the passenger seat. "I panicked, stopped the car and opened the doors," he explained.

In all, four full-blooded attacks were experienced and the rest of the time there were incidents but nowhere near as intense. He described to me an experience four days later when he was at an interview in a Northampton hotel and the chair next to him moved. Throughout these times he was researching into the history of the house to see if it had any bearing on the events.

"We were both depressed and falling out over stupid things,"he added.

Then on the Sunday they decided to go to the Spiritualist Church in Macclesfield and travelled in her car - which always had a full tank of petrol. When they were entering Macclesfield, a matter of about three miles, they ran out of petrol but managed to glide into the petrol station there. They filled up the tank and noticed one of the car's tyres was flat. Colin got out the jack but noticed the brace was missing. "We were being told not to go," he said.

When they arrived at the Church the service was nearly over and the Medium asked "Does wood mean anything?" Colin's father was a joiner and, said Colin, "The Medium told me things I did not wish to know. The Medium also said someone had died suddenly and did not know where to go . He told me, 'Tell it you love it and ask, if there is a good spirit nearby, would they please help.'

They returned home and sat in the lounge and decided to do as they had been told by the Medium. As they did so, said Colin "we both started to rise up in the air, a matter of a few inches, and there was a tingling feeling, like being tickled with feathers. Then it was like the best orgasm I had had in my life, rolling up the body and getting more and more intense and getting quicker and quicker. A pink turquoise mist formed round the television set and as we floated, the 'orgasms' kept coming. We felt we had to get out."

They left the house and went to the Harrington Arms at Bosley and later, brought two friends back to the house with them. There was nothing. The following day, a Monday, he went to work and decided that something would have to be done. He later telephoned the Samaritans and they put him in touch with the Church of England Cheshire Diocese who put him in touch with the Archdeacon of Macclesfield and then he telephoned the then Vicar of Wincle and Bosley, the Reverend Peter Barrett, who told him that there was a bible class on at that time but could they both, please, come up to the Vicarage at Wincle straight away. They went out to the car, there was a howling wind (it was the middle of February by then) and as they arrived the class had just finished and they went into the front room.

The Vicar's wife, Ruth, said: "You've got problems, haven't you?" and as she did so Colin felt the room they were in became elongated and distorted and he had to get out. He and his ladyfriend could not look at one another, they were both experiencing the same sensation and the Vicar and his wife said they would go to the house there and then.

Said Colin: "As we walked in the air was thick - like a pub tap room - and there was a smell as though someone had emptied a septic tank on the floor. The Vicar walked in and went into the front room and said "By the power invested in me by the Lord Jesus Christ I claim this house and the people in it." He went on his knees and prayed and, said Colin, the smell changed "from sewage to spring water," and added, "I had got belief - something to fight back with - and I had got my protection."

Two days later he was able to go back into the house on his own. He went into the bathroom and the mirrored door on the bathroom cabinet started to open and shut. "I was frightened of my own reflection in the mirror," he said. "I got to my knees and prayed and it stopped. I then felt something pushing me down and I prayed and it stopped. I was there for an hour and I was fighting back. It was a spiritual battle and I would not have been here now if I had not won."

It was after this that Colin started to study and, he said, he realised that there was 'a continual battle for souls between good and evil.' He said: "I used to be a real Jack the Lad but have since studied God's word and I have studied how to read the Bible." It was during one Bible Fellowship Class that he was told about the writings and work of E W Bullinger *Figures of Speech Used in the Bible,* Eyre and Spottiswood, 1898 and other similar works and has been an ardent follower ever since.

But the story does not end there. Shortly afterwards, a retired Minister of the Church made a visit to the house. He was what some would call an Exorcist and he was described as a lovely, down to earth man. He was accompanied by the Vicar of Wincle and his wife and they had a discussion in the front room about everything and anything - the weather, sport and much more. Then the retired Clergyman said "Right, lad, let's have a look," and walked to the stairs. When he got to the 'crossroads' at the top of the stairs he suddenly stopped and told Colin this was the main place where he had had the problems. He went from room to room and said that particular room was clear or there were still a few 'ripples'. He said Colin had experienced problems with the mirror and the cabinet, although he had not been told this, and in the study and dining room there had been no problems. This was correct. He walked down the corridor and into the front room and correctly said there had been problems there and when he came into the kitchen said things had been thrown about there. He explained about the 'ripples' and what Colin had experienced was the tail end of them.

Just before Colin concluded his story to me he said; "When something like this happens, people glorify evil. I want Christ to have that glory."

He then added a footnote - since then he had been actively engaged in theological studies but over recent times these had trailed off somewhat. Then one day his wife looked out of the window and noticed a man with a video camera taking shots of the house. He went out to find out why this was being done and got into conversation with the man, an elderly gentleman, and it transpired he had lived at the same house in the 1930s. "Has it still got the ghost?" asked the old man.

This Colin took to be a gentle jolt to continue his studies.

Ghost in silk stockings

Let us look at a few more tales of hauntings, and then let us find the common thread that binds them all, or so it appears.

As the traveller climbs out of Macclesfield towards Buxton there is, on the left hand side, a garden nursery called "One House Nursery" and here once stood a very special house. It was called the One House and probably derived its name because it was the

The One House before demolition. *Courtesy of Mr Harold Buxton*

main house or the only house - the one and only One House! It was also known as the Rainow Manor House and its history dates back to around 1166 when Richard de Davenport the main Forester of the Royal Hunting Forest of Macclesfield was given the house known as Anhus (One House).

A regular visitor to the house was a gentleman known as Mr Richard Knowles and he told the tale in 1936 that the lady of the house - most probably at that time Sarah Hulley - used to say the One House was haunted by a ghost dressed in short breeches, shoes with big buckles and silk stockings, rather like a royal courtier. He haunted the area to the front of the house and was to be seen walking up and down the driveway or, sometimes, around the outbuildings and stables. It has been recorded that at rather a grand dance one evening at Eddisbury Hall further down the road, conversation turned to this ghost and some of the guests were rather doubtful as to its existence and the lady of the One House became very angry.

Mr Knowles said "From 1903 onwards, I often paused to have a yarn about local history with an ancient farmer named John Oakes who lived with his son-in-law at Kerridge. For 16 years he had been coachman to Mr Jasper Hulley of the One House and when I asked him about the ghosts he said he knew of the tradition but although he was often out and about the place at night had never seen it."

Haunted by friend of the family

In March of 1990, the newspaper of which I was then the editor, the Macclesfield Express, reported that a beautiful lady in white had returned to haunt an eighteenth century Macclesfield house - fifty years after her last visitation.

The ghost was spotted early one morning by 62 years old Mildred Clewes, living in the old gamekeeper's house on Mason's

Lane, Hurdsfield. Mrs Clewes said: "I glanced at the doorway and saw this lady dressed all in white. She had a head scarf over her head, something like a nun's habit, but I could tell she was young, in her early 20s, and very, very pretty. She seemed quite agitated and was beckoning me towards her with her arms. But after a few seconds she just vanished." Mrs Clewes was not in the least bit frightened or concerned, she just lit up a cigarette and continued her morning. The reason for her nerveless calm was that the ghost was an old family friend! She was first spotted by Mildred's husband's sister in law in 1935 and then again three years later by that woman's daughter. Since then her haunting of the house has been family folklore.

Her footsteps treading the antique floors have been regularly heard and one night, though not visible, she tried to push Mildred's daughter out of bed. Mildred was reported as being glad to share her house with someone aside from her cats, "she's just a friend to me," she said.

Ghost of the roadway

In September of 1994, Kath Phillips of Walker Lane, Sutton, near Macclesfield, wrote to the editor of Stockport Heritage Magazine, Steve Cliffe, and he passed her letter on to me. Within its pages she told of a strange event that occurred outside Capesthorne Hall, the stately home of the Bromley Davenports, who were once Foresters of the Royal Hunting Forest of Macclesfield. Capesthorne Hall's own ghost has been well chronicled over the years and I well recall the late Sir Walter Bromley Davenport telling me of that strange lady at one time. However, Kath's experience was not concerning that particular phantom. She wrote that in 1980 she and her then husband both witnessed a strange happening. It was a sunny afternoon and near the gates of Capesthorne Hall on the main road they both saw a man in strange clothes cross the road without looking and in no hurry and make straight for the thick briar hedge on the opposite side, passing through it effortlessly. They were more amazed because there were no gaps in the hedge, which had a thick bank of nettles in front and a barbed wire fence. Her husband, being the driver, was stunned by the fact that the car stopped beyond his control which allowed the scene to take place without the man being run over, according to the correspondence. A car coming in the opposite direction also stopped and started when theirs did after the man had gone by.

Coincidentally, Steve Cliffe was kind enough to pass another letter on to me. This one was from Mr Gerald Whitwham of Cheadle Heath, Stockport, who had a strange story to relate concerning his brother who purchased a brand new house on the 'Ullswater' estate at Congleton. His letter said that back in the 1970s when his brother had just become owner of the house he - the writer - visited the house and first impressions were quite favourable apart from a strange feeling of gloom and a sense of that all was not well.

One afternoon his brother was in the garage working on his car when he felt someone was watching him. He turned round and saw what was described as a 'misty shape' hovering six or seven feet from the ground. The shape, wrote Mr Whitwham, was appearing to move within itself 'like somebody trying to burst a balloon, from the inside'. His feelings on seeing this were not of fear but more of mesmerism. In the next few months this reappeared six or seven times and was only visible to him until their mother visited the house and saw this misty object six or seven feet in the air and she described it just as her son had done. The family dog, a 'large and fearless alsation' was there and whined and cowered in the corner. The brother and his family later moved to Warrington.

There are many, many, stories I could recount of similar occurrences for I have been collecting and studying this sort of experience for many a year but, for the moment, will confine myself to just one more and here I quote from a Leek Times of 1935. The article referred to the road to Cheddleton from Leek, near to a spot called Birchall where the playing fields and golf course now are. It reads:

> It is said that there is 'something' in the road just beyond Little Birchall. Horses won't always pass it at night for they can see what the human eye cannot; and it is by the stopping and scaring of horses that the 'something' has made its presence felt. How old this legend is, one may, perhaps, guess.

But our forefathers, though they told the tales of the Moorlands to each other from age to age, never put their hands to writing if they could help it. The legend of the 'something' on the Cheddleton road may be centuries old. Let us go and see if we can find anything to notice. Sure enough in the hedge on the right had side of the road is the fluted shaft of an old cross. Was it part of Cornhill Cross that stood on the hill near the cemetery? There is one in Cheddleton churchyard very much like this fragment. This stone at Birchall is said to have been the spot where country farmers met Leek buyers in the time of the plague. About one hundred yards from this cross, and in the field behind it, there stood until some 35 years ago a large mound of earth and when it was dug was found to be made of huge stones and in the middle charred bones and a pot of earthenware. On either side, similar graves were found.

Visit by aliens?

There is just one more thread to be woven in our tapestry. It is a tale of a lady who has continually seen UFOs - unidentified flying objects - and has even seen beings from within these objects.

155

In 1979, a 67 years old lady, Gladys Stevenson, was at a friend's house in Bond Street, Macclesfield. She said afterwards: "I am a psychic and I felt there was something strange outside. At the bottom of the next door garden I saw this giant ten feet tall silver man with no face, just a dome-shaped head - no arms and no legs - just going straight down from a pair of giant shoulders. It was glistening all over, radiating, and all around the trees were lighting up in a red and silver square. I guessed this was caused by the electricity coming off the man." Gladys had seen unidentified flying objects before that occasion and she saw them afterwards - and on each occasion she described them as like golden balls in the sky.

So what have all these instances got in common? Well, there are the obvious ones - they all concern strange phenomena - but I have given these as examples to illustrate just one point - that all these sites are on earth energy lines.

I have noticed that each sighting has occurred on a pronounced earth energy line. I have made a point of checking with dowsing rods and on Ordnance Survey maps with a pendulum and there is strong confirmation that these lines are there where these 'beings' have been spotted. At Bosley, Capesthorne and Birchall near Leek there are also ancient burial mounds nearby.

All the sightings are different, although a couple involve figures floating, a couple involve animals being scared (this is never unusual - animals are far more psychic and aware of what is around us than the majority of human beings are) and there are other combinations of similarities. I could mention many more similar occurrences in other places up and down the Three Shires (the phantom coach near to Dieulacres Abbey for example, or the grey lady near to Buxton's famous well) but fear I would be too repetitious.

I just wonder whether the energy contained within the earth and manifesting itself along these lines has anything to do with these strange, unusual events. As usual, I leave you to decide.

Good hunting!

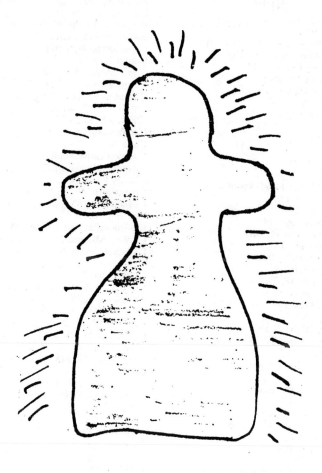

What Gladys saw.

Doug Pickford can be contacted care of the Publishers.

Earth Mysteries of the Three Shires

INDEX

158